T0381126

A Conversation about ...
The Eternal Life of Stuff

Two friends reflect on their journey through life
collecting stuff and finding meaning in it all.

BECKY CIVJAN AND TONY NAUROTH

BALBOA.PRESS
A DIVISION OF HAY HOUSE

Balboa Press books may be ordered through booksellers or by contacting:

Balboa Press
A Division of Hay House
1663 Liberty Drive
Bloomington, IN 47403
www.balboapress.com
844-682-1282

Because of the dynamic nature of the Internet, any web addresses or links contained in this book may have changed since publication and may no longer be valid. The views expressed in this work are solely those of the authors and do not necessarily reflect the views of the publisher, and the publisher hereby disclaims any responsibility for them.

The authors of this book do not dispense medical advice or prescribe the use of any technique as a form of treatment for physical, emotional, or medical problems without the advice of a physician, either directly or indirectly. The intent of the authors is only to offer information of a general nature to help you in your quest for emotional and spiritual well-being. In the event you use any of the information in this book for yourself, which is your constitutional right, the authors and the publisher assume no responsibility for your actions.

Any people depicted in stock imagery provided by Getty Images are models, and such images are being used for illustrative purposes only. Certain stock imagery © Getty Images.

All photos courtesy Becky Civjan and Tony Nauroth

Print information available on the last page.

ISBN: 979-8-7652-5184-3 (sc)
ISBN: 979-8-7652-5185-0 (e)

Library of Congress Control Number: 2024908536

Balboa Press rev. date: 05/08/2024

CONTENTS

(*Odd numbered chapters are written by Tony Nauroth; even numbers by Becky Civjan.)

A Conversation about ...

The Eternal Life of Stuff

By Becky Civjan and Tony Nauroth   *20 April 2024*

"Nothing can be so perfect while we possess it,
as it will seem when remembered."

– Oliver Wendell Holmes, Sr.
(American poet and physician)

PREFACE

The Seeds of Stuff

Becky Civjan and Tony Nauroth met through a common interest in writing. They joined a memoir group as strangers after attending a class at Northampton Community College near Bethlehem, Pennsylvania. It was taught by Jerry Waxler, whose book, "The Memoir Revolution," became an inspiration for them. Through Jerry, these scribbling strangers became friends, and neither wanted to stop learning when the class ended. Becky invited classmates to meet at her home in nearby Easton where about half a dozen enthusiasts, including Jerry as leader, shared recollections of their past.

But life gets busy, as it does, and the group disengaged for a bit, only to reassemble as an informal memoir "fan club," hosted once again by Jerry, at a local library.

When the Covid pandemic hit in 2020, their monthly in-person meetings screeched to a halt, but each member continued writing while isolated at home. Then, technology kicked in and the group re-grouped on Zoom to discuss their progress. It soon became apparent that they were unstoppable!

"Whether he wants us or not, Jerry is stuck with us forever," Becky messaged at the start of our first Zoom session when we were surprised to see the entire group show up eager to get started.

Sometimes one or another would disappear for a while. Life indeed got busy for them. That's exactly what happened to Becky when art lectures, workshops, and travel collided with the writing sessions.

"Three hundred sixty-five days a year, and everything I do falls on the same day," she wrote in an email to explain why she would miss several months of Zoom. "It's the story of my life. The minute I plan anything, it will collide with another planned activity."

Tony, meanwhile, didn't miss a single session. "I have no life," he said with his usual brand of humor.

Then, one day Becky showed up unexpectedly on Zoom, and it was like old times. The group continues to this day, sharing amusing, poignant, astounding, and sometimes disturbing memories.

"We grew into a family of sorts," Becky said, "encouraging and inspiring each other through individual personal commitment."

It was probably just a casual, half-joking remark that Becky unleashed one day between readings. It was prompted by coincidences that Becky and Tony share through a common bond – the United States Army. Tony is a veteran who served 20 years as a military journalist with his family by his side; Becky, her husband Ralph, and their three children lived for more than 29 years as a military family. Ralph worked as an Army dentist at many duty stations throughout the world.

After discovering that Tony was a journalist for the "Stars and Stripes" military newspaper for years overseas, Becky wondered if she had read some of what he had written, since that newspaper was her daily source of information for the eleven years she lived in Panama and Germany. Amazingly, it turned out that the Nauroths and the Civjans lived in many of the same places, although not at the same times. "How lucky we were," Becky said, "to explore different parts of the world, both geographically and culturally."

They grew up in the same era, with the same historical events happening throughout their lives. And now, in their mature years, they share a history, yet emerge from youth in different fashions with totally different memories. It's no wonder that their memoirs are filled with the same basic ingredients – people they've met from throughout the world who have influenced them, and STUFF collected from all points of the compass that grows in meaning and value as time goes by.

"Tony! We need to work on something together, you know – collaborate on something!" Becky exclaimed one day, and 25 exclamation points came flying out of her mouth (If you can't imagine this happening, then you really should meet Becky).

"That's a great idea!" Tony agreed, but it's the kind of thing people say without expecting it to take root. Still, it was an intriguing thought that lay dormant in their minds, waiting to be released like roses planted, but not yet in bloom.

The idea unfolded its first bud in July of 2023 when Tony discovered a box of love letters sent from his father to his mother before they were married in 1949. The letters had been squirreled away in the basement of Tony's brother's home in Factoryville, Pennsylvania. In an email exchange with Becky, he mentioned that he was working on what he hoped would become a book, "Love Letters from Leo."

Becky, who often spouts ideas in fountains of disjointed, yet incredible thought, mentioned that another good book along the same lines would be a collection of stories about the stuff people pack away in long-forgotten places.

"What happens to it?" Becky asked. And at that precise moment, she gave birth to "The Eternal Life of Stuff."

INTRODUCTION

Stuff We Talk About

The structure of this book requires a bit of explanation. Separately, Tony Nauroth and Becky Civjan have shuffled these stories together, like cards in a deck, but as a continuous conversation. Each story begins with a quote and ends with a comment from the following writer. We cover a wide range of stuff that we have collected over the years. It is in the form of adventures ... memories ... objects ... and mostly the stuff that matters most ... the stories of people who are swept into our lives and never forgotten ... the friendships ... the conversations ... the stuff that's so important to us all ...

Author Becky Civjan:
'My thoughts on the Eternal Nature of Stuff'

I love to move. I do. It is an invigorating and refreshing experience to see all our belongings being unloaded or loaded onto a moving van. I hold in my hand or gaze at objects I have collected throughout my life; then pause to wonder why I have not parted with some of them. How is it possible that some "stuff" can bring an emotional response just by its presence?

I opened my jewelry box, or rather my "box of precious stuff" the other day, and found the window cranks from my 1966 Turquoise Rambler American, my very first car. That car transported me through many memorable good times as I became a young adult, wife, mother, and world traveler! My treasured cranks are now obsolete antiques. This makes them even more valuable because I feel a history of change in the world – and in me – every time I see them.

Digging further into that box of treasures, I found an assortment of things that are absolutely of no value to anyone who should find them: three pennies tucked in a crocheted pouch, a cork, a heart-shaped rock, and a plastic square bearing a message in a foreign language.

Opening that box would give no one else a sense of good fortune, overwhelming good luck or well-being. That is because those items speak only to me about events in my life – moments from long ago that are mysteriously captured in each of these small mementos, telling me stories with no words, and communicating only through an emotional extrasensorial bond.

How can I ever part with this box of "Stuff" – stuff that prompts me to pause and remember those meaningful times from the past? Why would I ever want to?

Author Tony Nauroth:
'My Thoughts on the Gems of Stuff I Carry'

In his collection of short stories, "The Things They Carried," novelist Tim O'Brien writes about his time serving with the 23rd Infantry Division during the Vietnam War from 1969 to 1970. Part of what he reveals is that "civilized trappings" – the physical stuff we carry through life – are far less important than what we learn; what we remember.

That lesson comes to mind on days when I think about what the future holds for my prized possessions: my guitar, my home and land, my collection of business cards, my memoirs, journals, collection of beer mugs, and all the other bric-a-brac of my life.

Perhaps my family will organize a yard sale. Much will be given away. The land and house will undoubtedly be sold to help support my granddaughters when they go to college. Most of it, though – including my memoirs and my journals (kept since 1976) – will contribute a mighty weight to our local landfill. Or maybe not, and therein lies hope.

O'Brien wasn't writing about tangible things in his book – not "stuff." He was writing about things of the heart – from cowardice to courage – all less tangible, yet more important than "stuff." Still, while we are here, we covet stuff. We fill our homes with it; decorate our lives with this temporary tinsel, as if it's Christmas – year in, and year out; year after year after year …

We feel good when we acquire good stuff, great when it's great stuff, warm when it's hot stuff, trendy when it's trending stuff, and stunned when our stuff is just so much stunning junk. There might even be embarrassing stuff lurking in the darker corners of our homes. I say burn that stuff while you can.

Even if we're not joined at the hip with our stuff, when it disappears we wonder, "Where has it gone?" Whose life does it now fulfill (or just fill)? Or is it decomposing in a landfill? Or maybe it's appreciatively encased behind clean glass in a museum – for eons to come.

And how did this stuff come to us? What path did it take? What wide thoroughfare of our collective past has it strolled down in full display, perhaps to end up in a dead-end alley, in our own hands, or in memory only?

I am reminded of a passage in another book, "All the Light We Cannot See," by Anthony Doerr. He describes the thoughts of a World War II Nazi official, Sergeant Major Reinhold von Rumpel, who is on a single-minded quest to find the "Sea of Flames" gemstone, worth a fortune and said to have healing powers.

Von Rumpel notes that "… the fabled stone had caromed down through the pegs of history and dropped into my palm."

Isn't that the way of all stuff? It caroms through eternity in an erratic path, like a stainless steel ball bouncing through a pinball machine in a carnival game of chance. We can never predict which peg will send the ball in which direction. I thought the sergeant major had missed the boat. The real gem was the path taken by the "Sea of Flames," not the object itself; not the stuff.

Yet, even as I raise the flag of memory over the landscape of my stuff, I have to admit an uncomfortable truth – "Stuff" makes my gems of memory solid, well-faceted, real, and luminous.

So shine on, stuff! Shine on.

CHAPTER 1

A Calliope of Carnival Glass

Tony

"Everything being a constant carnival,
there is no carnival left."

– Victor Hugo
(Author, "Les Miserables")

Inside the second-hand shop of Tony's mom.

*O*h, how they sparkled! A fascination to behold. Row after row of various-sized glass canisters sitting on the shelves of a tall cabinet in our living room. But it wasn't see-through glass. It was like looking into a pail of milk fresh from the cow, but then zapped with rainbow colors possibly escaped from the Walt Disney animated movie "Fantasia." The canisters were squarish and tall, with fluted edges on top where the matching lids rested. And they were emblazoned with gold script advertising their contents: flour and sugar in the big ones; cinnamon spice and most things nice in the smaller ones. There must have been 20 of them, and if they could make music, it would sound like a carousel calliope. It's no wonder collectors called them "carnival glass." My mother never used them for their intended purposes. She used them as a decorative splash that lit up the living room. No need for lights when you have carnival glass shining down on you. Some would say these canisters looked garish in the otherwise subdued room, as if a carnival really had moved into our home, then exploded. But when my mother looked upon them, I think she heard angels singing.

Carnival glass is iridescent, coated to refract light which gives the glass a rainbow appearance similar to what appears on an oil slick or on the surface of bubbles kids blow out in the back yard on a sunny day.

According to an article on the Martha Stewart Living Web page, "How to Identify and Collect Carnival Glass," what we now know as carnival "was originally marketed under names like Iridescent, Pompeian, and Iridill as an inexpensive alternative to Tiffany Studios' costly hand blown favrile and opalescent art glass. One of carnival's many nicknames was 'poor man's Tiffany'."

My mother cleaned those shelves regularly, unwilling to relinquish the feather duster to anyone who might not kiss her prizes gently enough with it. Over time, one canister fell and shattered, leaving my mother also shattered for several days. And one or two lids also had losing battles with gravity. Another went missing. For weeks, my mother searched the house, scrubbing it down to the bones to make sure she hadn't overlooked its hiding place. But with six kids living under one roof, danger to those delicate delights was always close at hand.

Some of those jars, usually the larger ones, ended up holding stuff, like pencils and paper clips, and other random items. But my mother always made sure the set sparkled, at least on the outside. How could it not? It was carnival glass.

A few years later, my parents landed on hard times – I think it's an actual place. To make do, they rented a second-hand storefront on Main Street in Luzerne near Wilkes-Barre, Pennsylvania, to sell off our family's possessions, which were vast and numerous. That turned into a larger business in which my father would travel the byways throughout northeastern Pennsylvania in search of estate sales where all kinds of stuff could be picked up for a song. We all chipped in to clean, repair, restore, and re-purpose it for my mother to sell out of her shop.

One of the casualties of those times was her carnival glass collection. For months it rested on a table out of sight to all but the most determined of treasure seekers, and for a while she told customers, "That's not for sale. It's for display only." They usually gave her an odd look, as if to say, "Well, if it's for display, why is it hidden?"

Eventually, and perhaps because it was no longer in our house, the collection was sold. What broke my mother's heart was that buyers only wanted a few pieces here, a few over there, so they didn't just disappear in one fell swoop, they evaporated. Perhaps the flour canister went to a baker; the sugar might have landed in the kitchen of a sweet and much-loved grandmother; the salt could have gone to a sailor's boat; and a few of the spice jars probably went on display in the home of a newlywed couple.

Those brilliant shape-shifting colors baked into the glass of my mother's collection are the stuff of which dreams are made. Now her carnival collection is playing carousel tunes for new caretakers in parts unknown. Perhaps they're singing like angels.

*   *   *

(Tony, we have all sorts of memories from the past; some are dark and sad, others are bright and cheerful. Then there are those that sparkle with iridescence and glow in our hearts. I read a book with my book group called "Evidence of Things Unseen" by MaryAnn Wiggins. She mentions a mass of glowing iridescence in the corner of a room she describes, and immediately I could feel the intensity of that glow. Many years ago, while vacationing in the Outer Banks of North Carolina, we walked the beach at night, and, with every footstep in the sand, a spectacular glow appeared. I remember nothing about that vacation, but those footprints are imprinted on my memory. And then there are wonderful childhood thoughts of chasing fireflies at night. They flash so brightly among the pages in the scrapbook of my mind. Just thinking of radiant energy fills my brain with a bright turquoise glow! So, I do understand why your mom's carnival glass was sold, but I can see that those little rainbows of light remain in your memory. - Becky)

CHAPTER 2

Not Just a Table

Becky

*"The table is a meeting place, a gathering ground,
the source of sustenance and nourishment,
festivity, safety, and satisfaction."*

– Laurie Colwin
(Author, "Happy All the Time")

My nephew's wife and daughter standing at the table.

I decided to sell a table, a dining room table. It took a while and a good deal of soul-searching for me to place a photo and ad on the Lehigh Valley Bulletin Board announcing it was "For Sale."

"WHAT?" my husband Ralph exclaimed with eyebrows disappearing into his hairline. "You are selling our dining room table? The one we had made for us in Italy with the inlaid wood pattern that took weeks for you to design, and eight chairs so solid they can barely be lifted? The table that's the color of honey? The table we have used – extended to seat 12 – where we sat to celebrate engagement parties and wedding celebrations, and for countless years have polished off Thanksgiving Day turkey, gravy, and pumpkin pie with family and friends? THAT TABLE? THAT's THE ONE YOU'RE SELLING?"

The disbelief lingered long after he stomped out, shoulders raised and palms facing upward on outstretched arms. A perfect picture of dismay. I never thought of Ralph as being so emotional. I had asked myself those same questions, but still arrived at my decision. Chasing after him, and heading him off in the kitchen, I stared into his eyes which seemed to be spinning in his head.

"Yes … It's time. I thought about it long enough, and I don't like seeing that beautiful table in a dining room used so rarely, now that we have our tiny house in Florida to escape the dreadful Pennsylvania winters," I explained. "You know most holidays we celebrate are in winter. Our holiday cards now say 'HOLIDAY GREETINGS' above photos of our freshly built sandcastles at the beach." Then, sighing, I thought to myself, "What we didn't know at the time was this little motel-room-size house we imagined would provide us an escape from winter, became a place we did not want to leave at all."

There is something magical about our little house on Haverhill in the town known as Lakewood Ranch. We thought living in a 55-plus community meant we would have plenty of quiet time to sit poolside or at the beach, reading long novels, painting, or writing our memoirs. I envisioned a quiet … relaxing … lingering existence. The truth is that our retirement community is unbelievably vibrant and invigorating. Our calendars are filled with everything we love to do, and we certainly enjoy the endless summer. The truth is we needed to think about downsizing. Our goal was to say goodbye to "stuff" we no longer used or needed.

I was happy to get a call from a woman, Susan, asking if our dining room table was still available. She had seen the photo I posted online and thought she might be interested. She explained that she has a large family, they home-school their children and grandchildren, her 90-year-old father was coming to stay with them, and they could really use a large sturdy table. She came to look and said it was perfect.

The next day she arrived with her family to pick it up. When her husband took the table apart to put it on the truck, we saw the engraved name of the man who made the table for us in Vicenza. That is when I mentioned we had been living in Italy, and I asked if she had been there. Susan said yes, she had been to Rome twice when their choir was invited to sing in a church in Rome. She pulled out her cell phone and showed me a short video clip of their performance. As we stood outside watching the table being packed into the truck, Susan mentioned their choir would be singing this Sunday at a church in Allentown. She invited us to come hear their performance and said she would look for us. "It will be very crowded so get there early if you want a seat," were her words of advice.

We did go, and as we stood in a crowded doorway, Susan motioned for us to come to her pew where she whispered that she saved us seats. The sound of their voices woven into the service that morning was beyond wonderful. A young family sat in front of us. The pews were drenched in sunlight, and smiling children sitting next to their parents added yet another touch of beauty to the morning service.

As we were leaving, Susan mentioned that the family seated in front of us included her kids and grandkids. She asked if we would like to join them at her house for lunch. Unfortunately, we had to decline. After saying goodbye to Susan and her family, we filed out with the crowd.

I sent an email thanking Susan for inviting us to come to that lovely program and told her we enjoyed every minute. She wrote a note back saying she was happy that we came. She said right after the service her entire family met at her house for lunch and sat down at our table! She said everyone absolutely loves the table! I thought my heart would explode! I told her I felt sad when I posted the photo and ad to sell the table, but now I could not be happier, and I thanked her for that precious note.

*   *   *

(Becky ... Every once in a while, I regret getting rid of something precious, yet often that great unburdening is a cleansing of the soul as well as the home. And sometimes stripping our lives of the things we love leads us to new adventures and meaningful friends like Susan. Still, I can certainly see why Ralph was so upset and why you refer to this precious piece from Vicenza as "not just a table." – Tony)

CHAPTER 3

Shadow Boxing

Tony

*"Humans have a natural desire to preserve memories.
When we have an enjoyable, transformative, or unique experience,
a souvenir can act as a tangible memento of that moment in time."*

– Nilou Esmaeilpour,
(Founder of Lotus Therapy.)

Tony's shadow box.

*H*anging on the wall in my living room are three wooden display cases. Each is sectioned off into a myriad of tiny open boxes that allow light to illuminate the fronts of objects while throwing shadow over the other three sides of the items placed inside. Hence the name, shadow boxes.

One box is rectangular, containing 103 mini-box cubby holes. A square case holds 38 items. And the one shaped like a house offers just 25 spaces. That's 167 spots for my wife and me to show off souvenirs we've collected from our world travels, and during special events. They are reminders of life. And every single one of those spaces contains an object. We're running out of room. But imagine if we collected chairs!

It's difficult to collect sizable souvenirs when you're moving every three years from station to station in the military. Certainly, if I had continued to expand my rock collection (see Chapter 23), it would have become too cumbersome to carry with me, which means I would rarely get to view it. It would have been nothing more than stuff stuck in storage. As a solution, my wife and I decided long ago to pick up tiny items to display in a shadow box. That way, each one would trigger a memory of place, time, and experience – without the bulk. We do have a collection of sizable nutcrackers brought back from Germany. One is even four feet tall. But they are an exception and are more like room décor rather than memory placeholders.

The objects in our shadow boxes have little or no value. They're just a disorganized collection of knick-knacks and bric-a-brac shoved into whichever tiny compartments they might fit. Sometimes they barely fit. Other times they're glued in, to prevent them from falling behind the bookcase when the nearby front door is slammed shut, shaking the wall. Often, while deep cleaning the house, we discover those fallen memories.

We don't pick up mementos where we go – not in the way someone who collects ceramic thimbles from souvenir shops does. We pick up whatever strikes our fancy. Our favorite items are those that we literally pick up – just stuff lying around, often discarded garbage. Yet each is like a brain cell packed with memory and stuck in our shadow boxes – tiny skulls full of knowledge.

There's a silver replica of a radio tower, the symbol of Nuremberg, Germany where we were posted while with the "Stars and Stripes" newspaper. The real tower sits atop a now-closed landfill where a public park was created. They call it, without irony, "Mount Trashmore." Nearby is a tarnished brass belt buckle – too large for any of the compartments, so it sits atop the entire box. I bought it from an enterprising Soviet guard at the East German border back when there was a definite line in the sand between East and West. I gave him 20 Deutschmarks for it – worth about $5 at the time. It was a fortune for him. So much for the communist way of life.

The buckle sits between a small blue metal car, also from Germany, and a rubber shark larger than the car. That car is a model of the iconic East German-built Trabant, affectionately called the "Trabbie." It was the only car available in that communist country back in 1985, and it came in only three colors – gray, blue-gray, and off-white. If it broke down on the road, which it often did, its owner, or someone to stand in for him, had to remain with the car until help arrived. Otherwise, every Trabbie owner that drove by would stop and cannibalize the disabled car, because all Trabbie parts fit every other Trabbie – both a blessing and a curse. It wasn't looked upon as stealing, it was more like sharing. The door on my model used to open on tiny hinges. Fittingly, it's now broken, and I have no intention of getting it fixed, unless I find another model Trabbie to cannibalize!

The shark reminds us of how much Mary and I enjoy watching the movie "Jaws." We watch it often. Our daughter Bethany watched it once as a little girl, and it scared her out of her wits. She's still afraid of sharks, and her brother Ian will frequently pull the rubber monster from atop the shadow box and chase her around the house with it. At this writing, she's 50 years old, he's 46. He still antagonizes her with those formidable rubber teeth.

I have a shoulder patch tacked to the bottom edge of the box shaped like a house. It reads "USS Iowa." It was given to me by the captain of that battleship when it was deployed to the Baltic Sea east of Denmark. I spent a week on board, interviewing sailors and witnessing the firing of the ship's mighty 16-inch guns. The captain told me, "Those guns can hurl a shell that weighs as much as a Volkswagen more than 30 miles." Perhaps the weight of a Trabbie would have been more appropriate.

There are stolen items, I am ashamed to admit, like the pen I took from the counter at the "El Presidente" hotel in downtown La Paz, Bolivia. I wonder if it still writes, or if it even matters that it writes.

Over in the square shadow box is a small collection of cast iron figures doing simple, old-fashioned household chores – putting laundry through a wringer, cutting firewood, churning butter, etc. They belong to Mary, and they might be the most valuable pieces in the boxes. They also might be the only thing she was able to rescue from a childhood where any kind of stuff was rare.

A bright red cardinal is clipped to the top edge of the box, a reminder of how much Mary enjoys the many bird-themed items decorating our home. Next to it is a shot glass that belonged to my father. Every night he would come home from work, walk in the door, and go straight to the kitchen counter where he kept his bottle of cheap rot-gut "Ten High" whiskey next to the ancient art-deco toaster. He would pour himself a drink, carefully put the cap back on the bottle and push it back into its place, then down the shot in one gulp. Every night, one shot only. Then he would be ready for family time.

And how can I leave out the little pewter chipmunk, which seems to chatter on about a forest of memories from my years growing up while camping at Promised Land Lake in the Pocono Mountains, where chipmunks reign supreme? I can't look at it without thinking that if it had not been for my camping experience, I would never have met and married Mary.

Those mementos (Ian still calls them "men's toes") are a strange mix now. So many of them are there but have lost their connections to memory. Just stuff, and nothing more. Why is there a tiny green glass family group of swans swimming through three of the cubby holes, just taking up space? Where did the pair of pewter dice come from? Why is there a round red ball of foam squished into the top right square hole of the rectangular box? And what purpose does the miniature plaque – perhaps half-an-inch square – serve? It reads, "Blessed are the piece-makers." I can only surmise that it has something to do with sewing, in particular the little sewing circle that included Mary, her older sister Shirley, and her oldest sister Nancy. Sadly, both of her sisters have passed away. But that little plaque is still here.

Perhaps I should pull all those pieces out of their cubbies, clean the memory dust from the corners, separate the known from the unknown, and cull out the remembered from the forgotten. But after saving what's important, and leaving open space for new memories, what do I do with the stuff that's just stuff (albeit small stuff)? I suppose there's always "Mount Trashmore."

*   *   *

(Tony! Your trinkets speak only to you! If I were to walk into your house and see the display, I would think only that it is indeed an unusual collection of stuff. Now I can see as you describe each item on your shelves, that there is some reason you have kept these things. How lucky you are! It seems you have more mementos than memories! How lucky it would be to forget some of the memories attached to a collection of stuff; downsizing would be so much easier and less heart wrenching – Becky)

CHAPTER 4

Vicenza Villa Invasion

Becky

"Happiness resides not in possessions, not in gold, happiness dwells in the soul."

– Democritus
(Ancient Greek philosopher)

A beautiful villa.

*A*fter 29 years in the Army, Ralph began thinking about retirement and we began worrying about settling down. I could not imagine how terrible it would be to stay in one place forever. So, when a contract position with the U.S. Army in Vicenza, Italy became available, we put our retirement plans on hold, packed our suitcases, and headed for yet another exciting adventure.

On the top of Monte Berico, outside of Vicenza, stood a villa with a two-story apartment for rent. We briefly met with the owner. She lived in an apartment in Padua, and she and her family only came to the villa to spend time together on weekends.

We did not have much time to talk before signing the lease. The landlady seemed a bit aloof and stern. She insisted we not park in the parking area within the locked gates near our front door. She pointed off in the distance far below where there was a small area under a thin strip of corrugated plastic. Our car was broken into shortly afterward.

The next time we saw her was after we moved in, when she stopped by to inform us that, although we had no pets of our own, cleaning up after her dog would be one of our chores. A gardener worked at the villa. He did not like Americans at all and did not pretend to like us.

When the landlord's family came on weekends, large cushioned sofas were pulled right up to our front door on the patio we shared. We quickly closed the enormous wooden shutters on our front windows when we heard the voices outside. But by blocking out their festivities, we also blocked out any trace of light in our house. We could not leave with the front door blocked as well. After being stuck in the dark apartment the first time, we quickly learned to be gone early on weekends.

We paid little attention to the unfriendly atmosphere. Ralph was at work seeing patients, and I was busy taking Italian language classes. I particularly liked the language courses for "*stranieri*" (foreigners) because I made new friends from around the world. The University of Maryland credit courses on the Army base were great. I marveled at young soldiers who could not pass a quiz, could not distinguish a verb from a noun, but easily managed to pick up Italian girls AND win over their families, get engaged, and even marry before the semester ended.

After completing the language courses, I discovered that by taking the required history and government classes, one could get a Certificate of Italian Studies. I quickly signed us up, and we were well on our way to giving the longest, most boring tours of Venice and all that city's churches to friends, family, and even bystanders.

The most demanding and interesting course was on Saturday mornings from 8 a.m. until noon. We had courses in math, history, and geography, all taught entirely in Italian. I had seen it advertised on a bulletin board at the train station and could not wait to sign up both Ralph and me for the semester. It was a preparatory course to obtain an Italian GED certificate, which we didn't realize until the last day of class. No wonder it was so difficult.

Across the courtyard from us lived a couple who would walk their dog, a golden lab, every morning. The man was a surgeon, and both he and his wife worked at a private hospital at the end of our little road. Because of the rather hostile environment at the villa, I would manage only a shy little wave when they passed.

We had been in Italy for almost a year when Ralph and I returned from class one night and walked through our huge castle door. Ralph ran upstairs to change clothes, and I headed to the kitchen. As I walked into the dining room, I was annoyed to see that Ralph had left huge piles of papers on our table. I went to the staircase and yelled to ask him why in the world he left such a mess down here. Just as the words came out of my mouth, I heard his question for me. Why had I thrown everything from my underwear drawers onto our bed?

Even with those perfect clues, it took a few more minutes to process that we had been robbed. I called the police and knocked on the door of the Italian couple who lived across from us. In my best Italian, I told the lady who opened the door that "bandits had visited our house today." Well, understanding Italian is the easy part. Speaking and forming thoughts takes a while longer. She said her name was Marika, and she followed me back to our house.

The Military Police arrived with the local *polizia*. One of them presented us with a gigantic medieval lock that had been cut like butter out of a security gate and said, "This is how they entered." Everyone agreed the perpetrators were professional thieves.

We took a quick inventory of our home.

There was not one expensive item left in the entire house. Every camera, every piece of inherited jewelry was gone. They also grabbed the little safe we had not bothered to bolt down but were using to keep our passports and our plane tickets to visit our daughter the following week.

"Oh no," I sighed. "They even took that expensive area carpet we bought on our trip to Turkey," I said pointing to the bare living room floor.

The MP said most likely they did not want the rug but probably used it to carry away all the loot. That made me feel worse. He explained that it looked like they quickly grabbed everything and ran down the steep hill to the winding road below to a waiting getaway car. Feeling like the air had been knocked out of me for the fourth time that night, I managed a faint smile in response to his brilliant detective work. They left after leaving instructions to go to the station in the morning to fill out the police report.

Friends called to tell us how sad they were to hear about the robbery. My answer was always the same: "It's just stuff, and hey, I get to shop!" It was my way to get them out of their doom-and-gloom-sounding voices, and to lift my own spirits as well. The funniest response was from an Italian friend who told me not to take it personally.

"The robbers know you are Americans and have insurance. You can replace all your stuff at the PX (Post Exchange) with brand-new stuff. They can enjoy all your old stuff." She made it seem as though I owed the thieves a Thank You note for stealing from me.

I was glad we were not home when they robbed us and that no one was hurt. We certainly learned why people insure their jewelry. We had minimal coverage because, until the robbery, I had no idea how much those items, handed down from my family, were worth.

The day following the robbery, the landlady installed a security system in her part of the villa but refused to put one in our section. This prompted me to immediately look for another place to live that would be safer. On my way to find a real estate agent I stopped by the library on the post where I saw a friend from class. Teary-eyed, she told me that her husband was being transferred to Germany immediately. I could feel her sadness.

Then she explained they had rented a beautiful house in the small village of Dueville, and they were now forced to break the lease they had signed with the landlord who had been so wonderful to them. I leaned in to hear a little better because she could not possibly have said that. She repeated those same words. I then pulled out a chair for each of us, and we sat down to have a serious chat.

When I told her I was on my way to look for a place to live because we had been robbed and did not feel safe at Monte Berico, she invited me to follow her home and meet her landlord. This great coincidence grew into the greatest of times. The landlord, Roberto, and his family were wonderful. They even came to Pennsylvania to visit after we returned to the United States. They also traveled west in a motor home to explore the Grand Canyon and Yellowstone National Parks. Soon after standing on the edge of the Grand Canyon, Roberto's wife sent me an email describing that moment of discovery.

"Our mouths were wide open, but no words would come out."

That couple from across the courtyard at the villa became dear friends. We had great times together. When we were leaving Italy to return to the States, Marika told me she would email me in Italian every week so I would not forget the language I had struggled so hard to learn.

One of her emails years later warned us of a horrible virus that was killing so many in Vicenza. She explained it was very contagious and that it was best to avoid groups of people. She hoped that the sunshine and fresh air in Florida would keep us healthy. I double-checked every word with my Italian dictionary because the entire email made no sense to me until several weeks later when we heard – for the first time – the word COVID.

Sometimes I think of the day we were robbed at the villa in Vicenza. It seemed at the time that everything of value was carried away that day. The truth is, the thieves left things of much greater value. For without them, Ralph and I wouldn't have had those six wonderful years living in Dueville. In Italy we found friendships that are much more meaningful than the items we lost. Maybe those thieves DO deserve a thank-you note!

*   *   *

(Becky, I can't believe you took that loss so well. I also had an experience with a thief when a childhood friend stole "valuables" from me through his cheating ways. I responded by stealing from him what he took from me. I still can't decide which one of us was the worse thief. The incident ended in a knock-down, drag-out battle in my family's living room that my Mom had to break up. I'll never forget her pearls of wisdom when she reminded me that what we were fighting over was just stuff. – Tony)

CHAPTER 5

The Baseball Card Dust-up

Tony

"Every rascal is not a thief,
but every thief is a rascal."

– Aristotle
(Ancient Greek philosopher)

A floor full of flipped baseball cards.

*T*im Williams and I were good friends, although he could be overbearing and a little pushy at times. But he was my friend. We both attended Linden Street Elementary School in West Pittston, Pennsylvania; both in third grade.

Spring had come in 1958, and with it baseball season. And with baseball season came baseball cards – buying them, collecting them, favorite teams, best players, best positions, and the stick of bubble gum that happened to be included in every flat package of cards. But the very best thing about them was baseball card flipping.

It was something of a gambling game. Players, from two to as many as you wanted, would gather in little knots on the playground at recess. Each guy – for it always was guys – would grip a card with all four fingers resting on the top edge and the thumb braced against the bottom. With a flourish and a quick downward bent-wrist thrust, we flipped our cards simultaneously and watched them ride the air currents as they twirled to the ground, similar to throwing a curve ball from the pitcher's mound. We would call "heads" or "tails" and hope our cards matched our opponents'. Losers had to forfeit those fallen cards to the winners.

Tim's playing technique was to cheat. He would grab the cards before everyone had a chance to look them over, and he would simply claim victory. Nobody objected; he was bigger and meaner than any of us.

One day, I had had enough. After Tim cheated me out of almost a whole deck of baseball cards, I took action. At the end of the school day, I scrambled through the crowded halls to our lockers, which we were not allowed to lock, and fished all of Tim's ill-gotten statistic-laden cards, complete with players' photos, out of his locker. I shoved them into my pocket and started to leave.

Tim saw me grab them, but he was too far away to stop me. I ran. He ran after me. For six blocks, I hustled home as fast as my non-baseball-trained legs could hustle. Tim gained on me all the way. I burst through my front door just as Tim caught up to me, and we tumbled into the living room right in front of my mother who was watching a soap opera. We rolled around the room, throwing kid-size punches at each other and yelling and screaming. My mother was at a loss, and Tim, who was much stronger than I was, gained the upper hand. He swung his leg over my shoulders and came down hard on my upper neck with his butt, and I felt a powerful twinge of pain in my lower back.

I gave up.

When my mother recovered from the initial shock of this cock-fight, she, being much stronger than both of us, held us at arm's length.

"What's going on here?" she demanded. "Why are you two fighting?"

"He stole my baseball cards!" Tim yelled.

"You cheated them from me!" I countered.

The accusations flew, and so did ineffective fists. I think my mother just wanted to get Tim out of the house. She took the cards from me and gave them to him. Tim calmed down, my mother told him to go home, and then she turned to deal with me, but I got the first word in.

"Why did you take his side, Mommy?!"

"I didn't take his side," she said. "I stopped a fight. You're supposed to be friends. You were fighting over nothing."

She sent me to my room for me to "think about it."

"It wasn't about nothing," I grumbled. "It was about baseball cards," and I wondered why she couldn't see how important they were. One thing was certain. I knew I had lost a friend.

As I age, I face recurring bouts of lower back pain. I'm sure they stem from Tim's leap onto my neck all those years ago. I have changed my mind about what that fight was about. It didn't have anything to do with baseball cards, or "nothing" for that matter. It had to do with the indignity of being cheated out of my stuff.

* * *

(OUCH! Oh Tony I think the "indignity of being cheated, loss of stuff, AND personal injury" would have been too much for most of us to handle. I think you handled it well. Of course, I am surprised that Tim did not bring burglary charges against you for removing the cards from his locker. I guess this is a very good ending to this tale. – Becky)

CHAPTER 6

Flipping 'Floppy'

Becky

"If you feel pain, you are alive.
If you feel other people's pain, you are a human being."

– Leo Tolstoy
(Russian author of "War and Peace")

Holding tightly to Floppy.

*I*t was a very exciting day. My Uncle Henry, Aunt Lottie, and my two cousins, Rosa and Ella, were coming to visit us. They lived in New York, not far from the beaches, and it was always fun to visit them. They lived in a big house with a little boat moored at a dock in their backyard.

We lived in a very large apartment complex. Right outside the door of our building was a playground enclosed by a high chain-link fence. I went there every day. I could swing, see-saw, and go down the slide any time I wanted. It was an absolute paradise for an almost 6-year-old like me. I liked living there.

Our friends next door had bunk beds! I wanted a bunk bed so I could sleep on the top bunk, but my mom said I had the habit of waking up every morning on the floor because I tossed all over the place in my sleep. She said sleeping high up would not be a smart thing for me.

I was sitting on the swing waiting and waiting for our company to arrive. I liked being on that playground, especially when I was alone. I pretended to be a circus performer flying through the air when I was just swinging. One day, I decided to be a tightrope walker. I climbed onto the top of the chain-link fence and tried to balance myself and walk the perimeter. It was a pretty successful endeavor for about three steps. Then I lost my footing and went flying head-first down to the ground, which was hard.

The next thing I remember was a man in a dark suit carrying me into our apartment, and my mother was standing in the doorway staring at me, her eyes and mouth wide open – totally speechless. He put me down in the bathtub because blood was pouring down my face and over the back of my head. He said he saw me fall and that I needed to get to the hospital to make sure I was okay. My mother insisted I would be fine and he could leave. There was blood everywhere. My mother had a unique philosophy on health and felt that everything can heal naturally without being poked at by people in the medical field. I proved her right. I healed. Other than almost knocking my brains out, I continued to have uneventful days and years on that playground.

Finally, I saw a car pulling up to the curb. I jumped off my swing and ran to tell my parents. I was jumping up and down as the car stopped and my smiling Uncle Henry, with his steel blue eyes that matched the color of his car, greeted us with a big hello. My Aunt Lottie jumped out of the car waving and smiling. She looked like a movie star, because she always wore big black sunglasses and never took them off. She also wore bright red lipstick that ended up on everyone. We wore those kiss marks all day long all over our faces. She opened the door for my cousins and out they jumped, holding a HUGE stuffed rabbit with a big yellow bow on its neck and a stuffed toy carrot stitched to its hand. That rabbit seemed to be as big as me! I gasped and ran over to them and screamed with joy, hugging my cousins and the rabbit too. It was such a happy time.

I heard my aunt whisper, "Don't you have something to give to your cousin?" and both Rosa and Ella held out the rabbit and handed it to me. I kept looking at my aunt, and then back at my cousins, and they were all smiling. I said, "Mine?" and they said, "Yes."

I can't even describe what that felt like. I looked at the button eyes and embroidered nose of this rabbit and suddenly it seemed like it became REAL! I hugged it so tight my aunt said to be careful or I would squeeze the stuffing out of it. We all laughed.

My parents were busy talking to my aunt and uncle. My sister is four years older than I am so she never wants to be around me because I am "too young" she would say. She would rather stay with my parents than us little kids. My dad and Uncle Henry are brothers. They don't see each other very often, so when they do get together they have so many things to talk about. It's funny because my dad is quiet most of the time, but when he gets together with his brother, he is a different person and seems so happy. I wish we could live closer to family. We are the only ones in our whole family who moved away and settled in Washington, D.C. That's because when my dad got out of the service at the end of World War II, he was hired by the U.S. government to work with UNIVAC computers. These computers were huge machines with spinning reels of electromagnetic tape. They were kept in big, air-conditioned rooms at the Census Bureau.

My dad used to tell us about the unlimited possibilities of these machines. I can't even imagine how thrilled he would be if he were alive today to see computer chips at our fingertips bringing the world closer together and making our lives easier. Back in the late 1950's when he would talk about such an unimaginable world, well, to be honest, I thought he might be a little nutty. He died in 1973 at the age of 54. I wonder if he would have liked living in this computerized world he envisioned.

I loved growing up in Washington. We took the bus downtown to the Smithsonian and could stay there all day and not see everything in even one museum. There was so much interesting stuff to see, and I wanted to go there every day. My mom loved going to the Art Museums and I did too. I really wanted my aunt and uncle and cousins to move to D.C. to be closer to us. But then, when I think about the nice beaches they have close to their house and how we'd walk into town and drink egg creams all day, I guess visiting each other might be better than living next door. It is nice to experience different places. That's why people pack suitcases with stuff and travel.

We all went into the house. Our quiet home was suddenly full of voices and energy. My dad always liked to put a record on our record player, so music was playing in the background too. I ran into my room and pulled out some of my clothes to see if they might fit the rabbit. My cousins followed me.

"What should we call her?" I asked.

"YOU have to name her," they insisted.

I decided because her ears were flopping around, especially when I threw her in the air over my head, that I would call her Floppy.

Everyone agreed that was a good name.

We went out to the table for dinner and brought our food over to a little table set up especially for us. I pulled out a footstool and Floppy sat next to me. We offered her food, but she just liked the carrot she was holding.

I walked my cousins out to my playground, but we didn't get there because we heard the Good Humor truck and ran upstairs to get some money for ice cream bars and Popsicles. I left Floppy in my room to take a nap. Then my cousins and I took turns on the see-saw and the swings.

When we heard my dad at the door calling us, we knew it was time for them to leave. Everyone was slowly walking to the car to say goodbye. I ran upstairs and got Floppy off the bed to wave goodbye to everyone. I stood with my parents on the curb and watched as my uncle got into the driver's seat, and my cousins climbed into the back seat of the car and rolled down their windows. My aunt put a big kiss into her hand and waved it to all of us as she got into the car and rolled down her window. The sun was still shining, and the color of that car and my Uncle's eyes were so bright. It was the happiest day.

We heard the car start and with all windows rolled down we continued to exchange farewells. But, just as my uncle began to pull away from the curb, and I stood with Floppy's hand in my own hand waving big goodbyes, my cousins began to cry. The car stopped for a moment and my uncle looked in the back seat at his kids to make sure they were not hurt. The cries became louder and louder, and suddenly I heard my cousins yell, "We want Floppy to come home with us!" The cries got louder and we heard my aunt say, "Henry, let's go."

But the cries continued as they slowly pulled away from the curb … and … at that instant … my mother, who was standing next to me, reached over and pulled Floppy from my arms, lifted her over my head, and ran to the car, shoving the rabbit through the open window as they drove off.

I didn't cry or anything because I couldn't imagine that what happened really did happen. Finally, I looked at my mother and said, "Why did you do that?!" in such a loud voice it did not sound like me … and then the tears just flooded out of my eyes.

She looked a little surprised and said, "Don't be silly. We can always get another." I was not convinced we could ever find another Floppy.

I stomped back into the house hating everything and everybody and stayed like that for a long time. I sat in my room and complained to my doll Jackie-Boy about how mean my mother was to me and how I would never be that mean when I grew up.

My mother came into the room and tried to explain how important it is to always consider other people and their feelings. I knew she was right about that but what about MY feelings? She tried to tell me that the stuffed rabbit was not important. The important thing was that I made my cousins happy by giving it back to them. It made me feel a little better, but I still wanted the darn rabbit, even more than I wanted a bunk bed!

This was my very first lesson in the value of stuff. I could not understand fully at the time what she was trying to say, but over the years I learned to appreciate what she taught me that day.

How very odd, I don't have Floppy as a reminder, but I surely do remember the lesson ... and that day, filled with both happy and sad moments.

*   *   *

(Becky, that seemed so generous of you. It shows an appreciation for the right thing to do – and so early in your life. Sometimes we don't appreciate what we have until it's gone. It's even worse when someone takes it from us. That's what happened to me when my precious guitar was spirited away, leaving me "voiceless."

Note: Becky just told me that I misunderstood her large gesture as generosity. "But Tony," she explained, "I didn't give Floppy away. He was ripped away from me. I would not have been generous at all. That rabbit was mine and, in my mind, Floppy was Kidnapped!" – Tony)

CHAPTER 7

Cutting the Chord

Tony

"I am waiting for the lost music
to sound again in a new rebirth of wonder."

– Lawrence Ferlinghetti
(American poet & book publisher)

Tony's Gibson guitar.

hen I was assigned by the U.S. Army to attend the Defense Information School at Fort Benjamin Harrison, Indiana, I was filled with more than a little trepidation. I figured it would help if I carried something with me to provide familiar comfort to cushion my fears. Out of all the stuff I owned, I settled on my guitar.

My father bought it for me when I was 14 years old. It was a Gibson J-45 Dreadnaught acoustic guitar with a beautiful sunburst finish. It had a deep, resonating voice that reverberated throughout the room and along your vertebrate, especially within the register of its lower notes. My father bought it brand new for $189 at the Do-Re Music Store in Dallas, Pennsylvania. I know this because I happened to spot the receipt laying on his desk a couple days after my birthday. That guitar and me? We were inseparable, and the music we produced became an eloquent counterpoint to my usual shyness.

When I arrived at school, our class was told that the first order of business was to fill out heaps of paperwork and muddle through a number of other administrative tasks. The non-commissioned officer in charge of our group told us to pile our "suitcases and other crap" in an alcove near where our classrooms were located.

"You can pick it up at the end of the day," he said.

I raised my hand and he turned to me as if I was the third child in a kindergarten class to ask the same question.

"Yes?" he said, adding, "… and boys and girls, you don't have to raise your hand to speak here."

"What about my guitar?" I asked. "I don't want to leave it out in the open here."

"Don't worry," he pooh-poohed my concern. "We'll have a guard posted here," and he looked around at the entire class, seemingly challenging others to dare raise the same worrisome issue.

Feeling somewhat more comfortable about leaving my precious Gibson, but not entirely secure, I unslung its black canvas case from my shoulder, found an inconspicuous location behind a steam pipe, and set it on the floor nestled against a classmate's large backpack for a bit of camouflage. I reluctantly followed the group to a lime green and tan-ugly classroom where, for more than three hours, we completed paperwork and listened to instructors lay down the school rules.

When we returned, my guitar was gone.

I was in a panic, moving stuff around, searching in nearby niches, but it soon became obvious – someone had stolen my baby. I felt such intense loss and abject helplessness; I just knew I'd never see her again. And I was angry. The sergeant, however, showed no sign that he cared and blamed the loss entirely on me.

"What were you thinking, bringing a guitar to class, Private Nauroth?"

"I had no other place to keep it," I said, which was true. My family had yet to move into the trailer we had just rented and there wasn't any room in the truck for my wife Mary, daughter Bethany, me, the bare necessities for our new life, and my guitar, so I kept the guitar with me.

"Well, it's gone now," he said. "No use crying over spilled milk. We have work to do. Everyone back into the classroom."

"I'm not going," I said with a firmness that surprised me. "I'd like to report this theft to the JAG." I had paid attention to one of the instructors who had told us that the Judge Advocate General investigates the theft of soldiers' property. Never recognizing that I was using my guitar as a crutch to support the weakness in my confidence, I pretended that my loss was entirely financial. The sergeant stepped up to my nose and said, "Private Nauroth, right now your mission is to comply with your last lawful order, which is to complete your administrative duties in order to enter training at DINFOS. Do you understand?"

"Yes sergeant, but ..."

"DO YOU UNDERSTAND!?"

"Yes sergeant."

Again, we all filed back into the classroom, but the sergeant stopped me before I got through the doorway and asked, "By the way, private, how much is that guitar worth?"

A fellow musician once told me that I had a valuable guitar on my hands. I had researched its value and found that it keeps increasing as time goes by. The last time I checked was just before I went into Basic Training. Over the previous 13 years, my J-45 Dreadnought had appreciated in value quite a bit, so that's the figure I used.

"About $2,500," I said.

"Oh Jesus," he breathed.

For the rest of the afternoon, we filled out questionnaires, took tests, and responded to background checks. I, however, was not paying much attention. During the next break, the sergeant pulled me aside and pointed to the back corner of the classroom where a female lieutenant was sitting with an open briefcase.

"Private Nauroth, go back there and sit down. Talk to that officer about your guitar. You've got 15 minutes until your first class starts."

Curious, I went back and the officer introduced herself, adding "I'm from the JAG office. Sit down, I understand we're under the gun."

I was flabbergasted. Apparently, my sergeant had arranged for someone from JAG to immediately come to our building to help me solve my problem. Not only that, I soon learned that my sergeant had already outlined to her the whole story of what happened, although I still don't know what happened to the guard who was supposed to be on duty. She asked me all kinds of questions in rapid-fire succession, and then she hit the big one.

"Now, I understand this guitar is worth in the neighborhood of $2,500. Is that correct?"

"Yes, ma'am," I said, then I qualified it by adding, "according to current appreciation rates."

"I see," she said, which sounded a lot like I wasn't going to get enough money back to buy a strap for my Gibson, let alone the guitar itself. "So, how much did you actually pay for it when you originally bought it?"

I can't lie; my mother didn't bring me up that way. "I didn't buy it," I told the lieutenant. "My father bought it for me, but I know he paid $189 for it."

"So, in other words, you're trying to commit more than $2,000 in fraud against the United States Government."

"What? No!"

"I know this will hurt, but the truth is the Army doesn't pay for appreciation, only for depreciation, which means if your claim is upheld you'll probably get somewhat less than the $189 your father paid for it. And, since there is no paperwork to back up your claim, you're probably looking at the low end of what's possible. I'm sorry, but that's the way it is. In fact, you're lucky you got me; some investigators might recommend charging you with attempted grand larceny against the government."

"Whaaaat?" And then for some reason, I laughed. She didn't.

About a week later I was called to the disbursement office where I signed a receipt and picked up a check for $75. I also walked away with a new understanding of how the Army works. I also stopped playing guitar – in a sense, my voice silenced – for 25 years.

Instead, I turned to writing as a salve to my wound. Sure, I felt like I lost my voice when I lost that gift from my father, but as it turned out I didn't lose my voice at all; my voice simply changed. That guitar was just stuff. What was much more valuable was finding a more authentic vocal range in the written word.

*   *   *

(Tony, that is disheartening that something so valuable to you was taken in such a brutal way. I not only feel that horrible situation and the loss of that precious guitar – both monetarily and emotionally – but I can also feel your anger at being treated so unfairly. That must have been quite a bit to handle for a young man who signed up to serve his country.

However, during that horrible ordeal, you did discover something in you that has served you well over the years. Your voice in this piece that you have written has made us mindful of the importance of fairness in this world. If I were you, I would pick up a guitar today and write a song about it. I think using both vocal and musical talents would be the ultimate healing experience. There must still be a little bitterness even after all these passing years.

In contrast, Ralph and I had stuff that had absolutely no value at all for us but were surprised to find crowds of people who were thrilled to take possession of it. – Becky)

CHAPTER 8

An Impromptu Garage Sale

Becky

*"The answers may not be at the flea market,
but shouldn't we at least check?"*

– (From the "Petticoats of the Prairie" website)

Becky with a friendly helper.

After 34 years of moving around, we finally returned stateside and settled down in Easton, Pennsylvania. I discovered after five years that if I did not have a moving date written on my calendar there was no incentive to clean out a drawer or closet. Official Military Moving Dates were deadlines to get rid of stuff! I was spending a lot of time rearranging drawers so they would slide with ease. It's the price we pay for not getting rid of stuff.

In the Army, moving every three or four years had us on a perfect schedule. The ritual of cleaning out drawers and closets, with trips to Goodwill and donations to charities, made life clutter-free. Now I had nothing on the calendar to motivate me to tackle the growing emergence of Stuff! One morning I woke up and noticed we had an unbelievable amount. Some of the storage closets housed perfectly nice items, but since we had not looked at them for five years, it seemed to me that we no longer needed them. We also had a garage in need of a purge.

So early one beautiful, sunny Saturday morning, Ralph and I went out to the garage to see what we could cart off to Goodwill. Since the day was so pleasant, I brought a table and some chairs out to the driveway, so we could enjoy the sunshine while sorting through all the stuff. I dragged some old flowerpots and planters, and gardening tools outside to decide which ones we could use, and then carried out stacks of books, kitchen gadgets, clothing, art supplies; you name it, we had it. We took turns running into the house collecting anything else we wanted to banish from the premises.

Our van was parked at the end of the driveway ready to shuttle it all off to the nearest charity at the end of the day. It was fun emptying the closets. We found things we had not seen in years and wondered why we had kept them. A low wall lined our entire driveway area so we could stack all rejected items neatly along the top. I brought out another table and piled old pocketbooks, dumped costume jewelry and other smaller things on top. We were glad we got an early start. We had no idea we had this much to look through.

A woman driving by slowed her car to a stop and yelled down to us from her window, "Hey, are you having a garage sale?"

Ralph shook his head NO, but at the same time, I stopped what I was doing, thought for just a moment, and yelled back "YES!"

"Why not?" I whispered to Ralph. "We're out here anyway."

The woman came down the driveway and looked around. Ralph found a black magic marker and a piece of old poster board and wrote "Garage Sale," complete with an arrow. Then he put it out next to the street.

It took only a few minutes for another car to pull up. More women hopped out and ran to see what we were selling. Some folks came asking for specific items, and some just came to look and talk. It didn't matter to us. We were busy. We took turns running inside the house and hauling out more things like clothing, knick-knacks, dishes, pots and pans, books, and framed paintings.

The best part of this experience was that we were meeting new neighbors. Because our garage doors open and close with a remote, we almost never had to get out of our cars outside of our home. Even if we had met these neighbors, we wouldn't have had time to find out who they were.

One lady who lives around the corner came and saw the art supplies we were selling, then went home to get her husband who was an art teacher. They were a nice couple. We were talking about art when he mentioned that his main interest was African art. It made me think of a painting my sister had given to us when she and her husband came back from serving in the Peace Corps in Ethiopia in the 1960's. It was on a very large piece of canvas. I had it professionally framed and it hung in our homes for many years. But our style has changed from that time, and when I offered it back to my sister, who by then had switched from African themes to quilts, she declined my offer. The painting seemed to tell a story because of the small blocks of individual paintings within the larger piece. Over the years we had tried to decipher its meaning, but with little luck. I told our new neighbor to wait while I ran to retrieve that work, which we had unceremoniously dumped in the furnace room.

The art teacher was so totally intrigued by this painting, he called a friend who shared his interest in African art. He bought the painting and said he would let us know more about its story after his friend came to see it. We still need to follow up with him. It was uplifting just to find someone genuinely interested in this work of art and to know it was given a new life outside of a storage closet.

The day went on, and neighbors who enjoy gardening came to cart off all my old pots and planters and, well, others carted off just about everything else that lined our driveway. We were asked if we had furniture to sell. We did! We had a lot of furniture we were planning to part with. Out it went. Many of the shoppers asked if we were continuing the sale the next day.

"Sure, why not?" I thought, and we did.

It was the most successful garage sale imaginable. We enjoyed meeting the neighbors, and we never expected that cleaning out our house would be fun-filled and lucrative.

I guess instead of putting "Moving Day" on my calendar I could post a "Garage Sale Day" every year and clear out my closets and drawers on a "military type" schedule.

*　*　*

(Well Becky, that's one way to stumble into the garage sale business – and many people do try to run them as businesses. Sure, they can be both "monetarily and socially" lucrative, but sometimes they are also the stuff of dreams. My mother always wanted to own a high-end, second-hand shop. When she finally was able to open one, it became more like a PERMANENT garage sale. She used to wonder about the histories behind the pieces she sold and would often ask those who contributed to her inventory all kinds of questions: "Where did you get this? Was it your mother's? How old is it? What did this mean to you?" Then, when she sold that item in her shop, she would charge the customer according to the story she had learned about it, not according to its actual worth, although when she had a truly valuable piece, she went straight for the money. That's the way she was.

And I like to think she chose the name of her shop based on a mispronunciation of a strange new word I encountered when I was eight years old. – Tony)

40

CHAPTER 9

Antiques and Junque'

Tony

*"My mom passed on her obsession of all things
antique or vintage ... Treasure hunting is a family passion."*

– Zoey Deutch
(American actress)

The "Antiques and Junque" shop.

*A*t the end of our long driveway that curled away from our "House on the Hill" in Dallas, Pennsylvania, down through the woods, past the swamp, over the fields, and finally emptying onto Lower Demunds Road, sat a little home business with a strange sign out front.

"Antiques.".

For the first few days after we had moved some 15 miles from our previous home in West Pittston, I wondered what that sign meant. I had never seen one like it before. I was only in the third grade so my vocabulary had not yet fully blossomed. Each time I walked past it after getting off my new school bus, I tried to figure out this mystery. At first, I thought it must be the name of the older couple who lived there. But then I noticed that they got a lot of visitors who kept calling the man "Mr. Williams."

Each day I told myself I would ask my mother what that sign meant, but by the time I had walked up the driveway – looking for deer in the fields, searching for frogs in the swamp, watching chipmunks scamper among the forest trees – I had forgotten to ask. Finally, when the family was driving to some now-forgotten destination, we stopped at the end of the driveway to wait for a car to pass. I spotted the sign and immediately asked, "Mommy? What does 'ant-tea-cues' mean?"

"Ant-tea-cues?" she asked, with a bewildered look on her face. "I don't think it means anything."

"Then why is it on that sign over there?"

She looked, laughed, and then pronounced it correctly. "That's anTEEKS," she said, and explained that the Williams' bought and sold old stuff to make a living.

"Antiques are like junk," she added, "only it's really good junk."

"Oh," I said. "Well, why don't people just go buy new stuff?"

"Because sometimes the old stuff is better," my father chimed in. He was chuckling through this whole conversation; I was embarrassed, but edified. This moment would become a go-to memory for my parents when the family would engage in "Do you remember when ..." storytelling marathons.

That was about the time my mother started collecting antiques to fill our home with old things that made our surroundings new.

Decades later, after my father retired from the printing business, he fulfilled one of my mother's wishes – to open her own antique shop. They found an empty storefront property on Main Street in the small town of Luzerne, near Wilkes-Barre. I'd like to think that my experience with "ant-tea-cues" contributed to the name they chose for their new venture – "Antiques and Junque," for in their view, the stuff they sold wasn't junk. It was Junque – stuff with a college education.

*   *   *

(Tony, I never met your parents, but I feel that I know who they are. There was never a time in my life that I did not love taking a stroll down the aisles of a store selling a collection of items plucked from years ago when they were a part of someone's life; and lived long enough in that person's possession to fill the item with memories.

Those memories stay with the owner forever. It is what this book is about. The collection of memories through 'Stuff.'

People who have Antique Shops, Junk Shops, or maybe just huge barns filled with stuff, are selling so much more than the items they ring up in their cash registers. What they are selling holds a piece of history as well as a big chunk of emotional content.

How often, when strolling the aisles, do we hear customers like me saying things like, "Oh my gosh, I had one of those as a child." Or "My grandmother used that in her kitchen!"

We never lived in a place long enough to open a shop, but I think I would have loved to have a little place called "Becky's Book, Antique & Coffee Shop" where I could witness the bringing together of people with the "stuff" that enhances their warehouses of memories just a little bit more! – Becky)

CHAPTER 10

The Green Monster

Becky

*"The green oak and cedar – the dark pine,
the yellow and silvery-barked willow – each majestic old tree;
hath its own peculiar tone and whisper for thine ear."*

*– Elizabeth Jessup Eames
(Early 19th century American poet)*

The Green Monster.

I met Sofia in the grocery store in Enterprise, Alabama in 1982. There was an energy about her, and we soon became good friends. Her son was about the age of my two youngest, and her husband and mine were both assigned to nearby Fort Rucker (since then renamed Fort Novosel).

She was from Germany, and I remember the first time I walked into her house I was fascinated by the beautiful display of antiques. It looked like a museum to me. I loved her German wardrobes and tables from the early 1800s, glowing gold in the sunlight. I told her how much I loved her furniture.

"I refinished them," she said proudly. "It's my hobby. I can show you how."

"When?" I asked eagerly, quickly adding, "I'm not doing anything tomorrow."

The next day we went off to an old barn owned by someone she knew. It housed an enormous inventory of everything from fine antiques to junk.

"There are beautiful treasures hidden under layers of dust," she whispered as we walked into the barn. She went straight to the back wall and began working her way to the front, turning things over to see the bottom and rubbing off dust with a cloth. I stayed in the entry kind of stunned to see so many things all together – one huge tangle of stuff!

Sofia finished her search through the endless ocean of assorted furniture, picture frames, and old rusting farm implements, pulling out potential treasures along the way. She came over and looked at me as I stood staring at a very old, very large dark green wardrobe that looked as if it had housed several generations of rabbits. It stood about 6 feet tall, 5 wide, and 21 inches deep, with a lot of character and a primitive, hand-made appearance. When the owner saw me opening the doors and peeking inside, he laughed and said he would take anything for it. I too laughed. "OK," I said, "how about $40." To my surprise he grabbed it! I named it the Green Monster. Little did I know that when I opened that creaky old green door and peeked inside, I would find a whole new wonderful world of non-stop adventure.

The next day Sofia and I loaded it onto her husband's truck and placed it in my backyard. Sofia rolled up her sleeves and taught me everything she knew about refinishing. For months, we practically lived in my yard with the Monster. As the green paint dissolved, a gorgeous, aged hardwood wardrobe appeared and literally took my breath away. It still retained a hint of the green tint, which made it even more unique. In the final stage of its restoration, I had just finished vigorously rubbing it down with several applications of furniture wax.

"I'm done!" I yelled.

Sofia inspected the Monster and announced that it needed a little more fine-sanding and buffing. My instructions were to make it as smooth as a baby's butt. Once the Monster was completed and stood proudly in my living room, I could not wait to search for my next project.

We did a lot of trunks and blanket chests. I lined the chests in fabric and polished the metal trim of steamer trunks until they sparkled. Every trunk had a different design so there were many different techniques required. We had steel brushes to polish the metallic raised designs on the top of some; others had leather straps that needed replacing. I cannot even explain how much fun it was to learn so many things every day and how generous my friend was with her time and expertise.

The sad part about the military is that everyone is in a constant state of moving, and we part with good friends when they are off to another duty station. Before she left, Sofia introduced me to a man who owned a large antique shop in town. He had a professional workshop complete with a dipping table. The building was a barn-like structure nestled on a wooded lot not far from town. The first time I went to meet him, he had a shipment of furniture from England in the entrance.

"They're pub tables," he said, and reached over to slide one out to show me how easily they transformed into seating for six. "They are very popular. We can't keep them in stock. I am trying to hurry and refinish this new shipment and get them to my customers." I asked if I could come watch him do the restorations. "Sure," he said." I was thrilled.

That poor man could not get rid of me. I raced over every day for a few hours to learn everything I could. We refinished lots of pub tables and vanities from England. We fixed wobbly chairs and turned old wooden junk into fine furniture with such luster and radiance I wanted to keep every item that we completed! As the months went by, I felt I really knew what I was doing and was thankful for all the instruction I had received.

Another person Sofia introduced me to before she moved was an 86-year-old woman, Mrs. Clark. She and her son would jump in their truck and drive far out into the countryside, knocking on doors of homes and asking if the owners had any pie safes, quilts, or knick-knacks for sale. When she and her son returned with their truck groaning under a load of newly acquired stuff, the woman would call Sofia who would pick me up and we would hurry over to see the new batch of old dusty items. It brought to mind the old saying that one person's trash is another person's treasure.

On one such return I asked, "How in the world do you find the energy to do this strenuous work?" I even inquired about what magical food she eats for breakfast that would give her such energy and keep her so young.

"A shot of whiskey every day," she said, "and do not EVER sit in a rocking chair." She explained that all her neighbors are stuck in those chairs and hardly move anymore.

Our three years living in Enterprise, Alabama flew by, and we left in 1986 to move to Nuremberg Germany where we would stay for five years. I hit the ground running to every old barn and flea market and furnished our entire house in pine and golden oak pieces that I refinished myself. It was during this tour of duty that I discovered old barns filled with treasures buried under layers of dust and cobwebs. I actually spoke to the proprietors in German. It was the most fun and the most fulfilling time in my life. I turned junk into radiantly glowing furniture just like Sofia's! I refinished many wardrobes. The German's call them *Schranks* (rhymes with "honks," and note that Germans capitalize all nouns). I loved them all, but none ever captivated my affection the way The Green Monster did.

One day our 10-year-old daughter, deep in thought, asked me why we got rid of all their new possessions and started living with "all this old stuff." I told her that there is a charm to old furniture. When wood is buffed and waxed it seems to come to life. And when something destined for the junkyard becomes part of your most cherished possessions, it elevates the hobby of furniture restoration to a whole new level. The Green Monster is not just a piece of furniture. There is a dynamic energy that radiates from its smooth, glowing wood, and when I touch it, I feel Sofia's presence and I am reminded of our friendship.

*   *   *

(Becky, your friendship with Sofia is such a great example of how stuff acts as a spark to memory. Your story makes me want to meet Sofia. On the other hand, sometimes there are "friends" in your life who you never want to meet again! Let me explain. – Tony)

CHAPTER 11

The Clueless Shoeless

Tony

*"It is morally wrong to allow
a sucker to keep his money."*

– W.C. Fields
(Actor and stand-up comic)

Shoes dangerously close to a storm drain.

*P*art of my character can be summed up in one word – gullible. I can think of many instances to illustrate this self-assessment, but when one in particular comes to mind, it arrives like a rubber flip-flop that slips off my foot underwater and rockets to the surface.

My early years were spent in a half-double home in West Pittston, Pennsylvania on a wide tree-lined street with good-size yards and lots of kids. It was the end of August in 1958, and me and my five siblings were thinking about the approaching school year. I was probably headed into second or third grade. One of our annual rituals was going to a shoemaker's shop in Pittston, just across the Susquehanna River. It was a time when there actually were cobblers, no longer a job title, it seems; gone the way of all those other jobs; their shingles that once advertised their trades disappeared with all the other vestigial trappings of history – stuff turned to dust.

But at the time, a new school year demanded new shoes. It was the last shopping day before classes began, probably a Saturday morning. All six of us traipsed into the shop where we were greeted by the owner who reminded me of Geppetto, of Pinocchio fame. He was always happy to see us (or perhaps, more to the point, our 12 feet). We were measured and given choices of various footwear; and there were the turned up noses at patent leathers and "sissy shoes." It was a drawn-out process that took hours from the time we left our house to the time we came back to show Mommy our new footwear.

After the excitement wore off, we asked her if we could wear our shoes outside before supper. She hesitated, but then said, "Okay, but only for a few minutes, and don't go into the sandbox." We had a big old sandbox out back. We told her we just wanted to show our shoes to our friend Denny Jameson, who lived across the street. "Okay, but come right back. And stay out of the puddles!" It had been raining off and on since the morning, but the sky was now clear.

As we scrambled out the door, we yelled, "We will!" over our shoulders, and, clicking our heels, we marched over to show Denny our new shoes.

Now if Denny hadn't been sitting on the curb on our side of the street, perhaps the rest of this story wouldn't even count as a rocketing flip-flop kind of memory. Denny, who was a few years older than me, was poking a stick at a storm drain grate and I believe he was contemplating physics. We all said hi, what's new, and what do you think about school, and then the subject of our new shoes "happened" to come up. We showed them off with great pride. Then Denny dropped the stick through the grate, and it splashed into the rain-swollen stream below. Denny's face brightened and he said, "Say, did you know that this storm drain is connected to your house? And if you throw something down here it will come up out of your toilet?"

We seriously doubted this and let Denny know so. However, he was older and knew a lot more than we did about such stuff.

"But how do we know it's not true?" he asked.

Well, being elementary school kids, we were unaware of the dangers of trying to prove a negative, so his question seemed reasonable. And eventually, at Denny's behest, we decided to conduct an experiment, but could find no readily available second stick. We finally agreed that the only reasonable solution was to – you guessed it – throw a new shoe down. But not just one shoe. we went all in; all 12 shoes went into oblivion. What should have tipped us off to Denny's perverse plan was plain enough – he kept his shoes on his feet, but we were oblivious, taken in by this grifter's charm.

As splash followed splash, Denny laughed like a donkey, hee-hawing all the way over to his house. Meanwhile, we ran back up our sidewalk, over the porch, through the door, and upstairs to the bathroom where we stood expectantly around the toilet – in our stocking feet.

Nothing happened.

"Maybe we have to flush," my brother David suggested.

I flushed.

Nothing.

We tried it again.

Nothing, and then we began to worry.

My mother, curious about all the commotion at the commode, asked what we were up to. It was dawning on us that we were up to our shoelaces in trouble, if we had had any shoelaces. After we explained about the experiment, Mommy, in her lilting voice that always seemed a prelude to trouble, called to Daddy, "Oh Leo ... !" (with added emphasis on the first syllable of his name).

After my father listened to our story of self-inflicted woe, he was mad as hell. In retrospect, I think he was more angry that we had been such suckers.

It was late afternoon, and now we needed new shoes – again. Daddy rushed to the phone to call "Geppetto," briefly explained what had happened, and asked if the store could stay open for us. Geppetto, who knew how to count to 24 shoes, readily agreed. We rushed over to experience the annual shoe-shopping ritual for the second time on the same day.

Later, my father pulled us aside to explain the meaning of the word "gullible". I'm pretty sure he also had words with Denny's father. This wasn't the first, and not the last, time I fell for something, and each time that flip-flop burst through the surface of my thoughts, I cringe at how I had been duped. Still, this is the kind of thing that puts shoe leather on the stuff of memory.

*　*　*

(Tony, I think you and your siblings gave the word "Gullible" a whole new meaning! You know, I just happened to have lived very close to a shoe store when I was growing up. One day, inside the store, a big machine that measured our feet also allowed us to actually see our bones. I was thrilled. It was so exciting I marched into that shoe store every day just to look at my feet.

Speaking of feet, did I ever tell you that I once dreamed of being a Rockette one day, dancing my heart out at Radio City Music Hall in New York City? I even told my first-grade teacher. But practicing high kicks and splits was exhausting, and hurt, so I changed my mind by second grade. Still, the thought of dancing every day stayed with me, because it lifts my spirits and makes me smile. – Becky)

CHAPTER 12

Happily Dancing Through the Years

Becky

"You dance joy! You dance love! You dance dreams!"

– Gene Kelly
(Dancer, choreographer, and film star)

Dancing through the years.

I came across a tiny pin with a dancer on it the other day when I was looking for something in my jewelry box. Imagine how many years I have kept that pin. It was given to me by my dance instructor at my first tap recital when I was four in 1952.

I will never forget that recital or the costume. It was kind of a white satin bathing suit, and a tuxedo-like jacket with tails down the back, and thickly covered with gold glitter. A satin bow tie under my baby double chin and a gold top hat completed the look. Our mothers had to wrestle with so many snaps and hooks to get us dressed. It was quite time-consuming, and the minute all was in place, everyone in my class, including me, had to use the bathroom at once.

On the day of the performance, our mothers dabbed our faces with lipstick, a bit of blue eye shadow, and rouge on our cheeks. Then they sent us through a thick velvet curtain and out onto the stage with lots of lights. In front, below us, sat the audience waiting to be entertained. Our hearts raced as we put on our show, listened to the applause, took our bows, held onto our top hats, and ran off the stage with our tap shoes slipping and sliding on the polished floor.

It is memorable when a child feels that kind of excitement. Life was kind of boring off that stage. Dance was invigorating and made me feel good. It still does.

I entered a poetry contest when I was about eight. I think it was around Valentine's Day, and the topic was love. I immediately knew I would write about dancing. In my poem I said that when I put on my dancing shoes the whole world was a happy place!

I wrote lots of poems after winning that contest. I carried them around in a little book. My mom used to ask to read them and liked them. I hate to admit this, but one day I got mad at my mother and I ripped up that book and threw it in the garbage can. The next day I couldn't even remember why I was so angry, but when I went to the garbage bin, it was empty, which meant the garbage men had already picked it up and it was gone forever. What a great lesson for me to learn! Do not do anything drastic when angry. It is a lesson I will never forget.

I gave up dance classes in my teens after dancing on stage at Atlantic City's Steel Pier with Xavier Cugat, Charo, and the diving horse. I keep my pair of silver tap shoes to dance around the garage for exercise. It is a great workout. Shoes take up less room than a treadmill, and dancing is more fun than lifting weights or running.

I happily Twisted, Mash-Potatoed, Strolled, and Cha-chaed my way through high school dances and teen clubs. I raced home from school to watch Dick Clark's "American Bandstand" and danced in front of the TV. Together with friends we figured out the steps.

I was born in 1948. Consequently, I became enchanted with the 1960's Go-Go Dancers and later, Disco. Those great times made me feel like that kid in tap shoes dancing on the stage again.

In today's world, we recognize things like a "runner's high." We understand the brain can produce endorphins that bind to opioid receptors. We know that endorphins can:

1. reduce pain,
2. boost happiness and pleasure,
3. reduce stress and anxiety,
4. reduce depression.

That explains why I like to dance, and will never stop!

In 1996, when we were assigned by the Army to Hawaii, I took Hawaiian dance. On Friday afternoons we entertained tourists poolside at a Waikiki Hotel. We also danced on the beach at sunset. The sound of a conch shell blown at dusk would announce the beginning of the show. We were also thrilled to dance at the Waikiki Shell, an outdoor performance stage. Hula classes are wonderful because the families who have been teaching for generations take it very seriously. Learning the Hawaiian culture is as important as learning the steps and motions. It is a beautiful, flowing style of dance, and there is something spiritual you feel when you do the movements.

When Ralph and I married, I decided it would be fun to buy each other "lessons" instead of wrapped gifts for birthdays and anniversaries. It cut down the amount of STUFF we accumulated. I have gifted him with German, Spanish, Sign Language, guitar, sewing, and writing classes ... and more.

We entered the empty-nest part of our life when we moved to Hawaii and I signed Ralph up for Ballroom Dance classes on his birthday. He was not thrilled. He said there was no way he was going to learn to dance and yelled, "Becky, I have size 12 flat feet and am uncoordinated and I am absolutely not going!" He looked so cute, like a little boy refusing to brush his teeth. I sat him down and explained that it was a PRESENT and he could not give it back. It was a gift. It was his. It could not be returned to me. We were indeed going to learn to dance – together!

I had to physically push him into the car and drive him over to the school gym where the dance lessons were taught. He would not budge from the passenger seat. He explained that he was having flashbacks to eighth-grade gym class dance lessons. It must have been truly traumatic for him.

I pulled him out of the car. We walked into the building, down a long corridor, and into the gym. A large group of students were gathered near the doorway, signing the register. Most of the people were from the Philippines and small like me. At 6-foot, 2-inches, Ralph towered over everyone there. I felt sorry for him, but I wasn't going to cave in to his awkwardness.

The dance classes were surprisingly enjoyable for both of us. We had a great time; learned the steps; made new friends and had fun. At a potluck dinner after the first semester, Ralph discovered that our Filipino classmates were excellent cooks. He immediately signed us up for more classes. Thank heavens for those potlucks!

Ralph retired from the military, and we lived in Vicenza, Italy for six years and finally settled down in Easton, Pennsylvania. Settling did not last long.

In 2019 we bought what we thought would be a tiny little Florida winter house in a 55-plus community. What we did not expect was to find an unbelievable number of social things to do. We signed up immediately for karate/self-defense, Pickleball, Bocce, Zumba,

Watercolor and Acrylic Art, and Ballroom Dance. I even volunteered to lead a Book Club! We were so busy and having so much fun we never wanted to leave! We now stay year-round.

AND THEN ... One day I was looking through our community newsletter and I saw an ad written by a retired dance teacher who wanted to know if anyone would be interested in tap lessons. I was the only one to sign up.

A few months later she put the ad in again. When there were three of us the lessons began! We have 18 tappers in the class now, and we are having such fun. Some things come back to us very fast. Sometimes finding your right heel and left toe, then left heel and right toe, is not as simple a task as it was when we were young; and fitting those tapping sounds to the beat of the music leaves us a little more breathless than I had remembered. Still, the steps do come back to us and we rarely miss a beat. We feel young again. It's fun, it's exciting and exhilarating ... and it makes our ordinary world ... a stage!

*   *   *

(Becky, it's amazing how shoes help us get around. Sometimes toys also transport us to fun places. However, I once learned that when you pick up a yo-yo at your favorite store before you learn to "walk the dog" – a tricky yo-yo maneuver – you shouldn't play tricks with your responsibilities. Check it out, and don't do what I did! – Tony)

CHAPTER 13

Fourteen Yo-yos and a Guilt Trip

Tony

"The number one rule of thieves
is that nothing is too small to steal."

– Jimmy Breslin
(Journalist and columnist)

Yo-yos of joy and remorse.

*T*here comes a time in a boy's life when he needs a Yo-yo. Learning to do tricks with one is a rite of passage for the preteen set, and sometimes the ritual spins right on into adulthood. But it begins as a childhood calling.

All the other kids among our group of campers at Promised Land State Park had Yo-yos. Why not me? The question was critical, for without a Yo-yo, I would be without my friends. I would be … outside.

I'm not sure what drew me to the Pine Cone Gift Shop in the Pocono Mountains that day in 1964 when I was 14 years old. It's true that I would stop there occasionally while riding my bicycle from the lake's beach to our campsite, but I didn't have money to buy anything other than an occasional soda or candy bar. Sometimes I just stopped there for a rest, but I did like to wander through the store looking at all the souvenirs the tourists would seek – little stuffed bears, chipmunk key chains, plaques that bore sayings like, "Camping is when you pay a fortune to live like a homeless person." And of course, there were obligatory T-shirts with pictures of the lake surrounded by pine trees, and "Welcome to the Promised Land" written on them. My favorite aisle, however, was where the toys lived.

One summer day, while the other kids were out playing with their Yo-yos, negotiating maneuvers like "walking the dog," and "cat in the cradle," and negotiating for each other's Yo-yos, I was by myself in the gift shop. The place always smelled of artificial pine-scented incense and freshly brewed coffee. I was in the wrong place, looking at what I thought was just a bunch of useless touristy stuff. Yet, someone was always in the shop, looking for mementos they would value as a reminder of their vacation in the Poconos.

I found myself in the back aisle, in front of a display case, staring at a whole bin full of Duncan Yo-yos – the top line among those in the Yo-yo know. I stared at them, eyes full of longing, but a wallet empty of cash.

All those Yo-yos! Wow! I had to have one. I knew that my next move was wrong. I should have remembered that my parents raised me right. But I HAD TO HAVE A YO-YO.

I moved close to the bin, checked the aisle, left then right, and I surreptitiously slipped a cobalt blue yo-yo into my pocket. Despite hearing my mother's disappointed voice in my ear, I backed away and pretended to look at other toys, but without actually seeing them. I was nonchalant; I may have even tried to whistle, although I never was able to do so. I could only blow a stream of hot air. I sauntered out of the gift shop, hurried over to my bicycle, checked to make sure no one was looking, and slipped my stolen prize into the bike's saddlebag. That almost seemed too easy. Then I got another bright idea.

"If one Yo-yo is good, two would be even better."

I now had shoplifting experience. I knew what was possible. I returned to the gift shop, back to the toy aisle. Look left, look right, and ... snatch! Another one in my pocket. Instead of moving away, this time I continued to look at the bin. There were red ones and green ones, and yellow and black ones, and the two I took barely reduced the size of the pile.

"They won't even be missed," I thought. I grabbed some more, stuffing them into my jacket and pants pockets. Hand over fist I went, scrambling before someone could spot me, all the while knowing this was wrong, but driven by the siren call of the Yo-yo, urging me to take, take, take what was not mine.

I strode confidently, but probably looking a little too lumpy, out the door, my pockets bulging with 13 more yo-yos. I stuffed them in my saddlebags and rode off into the sunset, feeling like an Old West bank robber who had tricked the short arm of the law.

When I got to my family's campsite, I hid my pirated booty, took two of the Yo-yos, and went in search of my friends. I had a lot of dog walking and cat cradling to catch up on.

I don't know what happened to all that contraband. I think I gave some away, but I might have sold a few too. I know I broke at least two – kids tend to be less careful with stuff that isn't theirs.

As the days ground on, my moral upbringing grew more present every time I played with one of those Yo-yos, and the shared rituals associated with possessing a Yo-yo diminished as my friends and I naturally went our separate ways. My shame as an undiscovered thief, however, swelled to gigantic proportions, especially with each Sunday when I went to church. The days spun into weeks, and then months. Yo-yo season came and went, and the guilt piled up, making me feel ever more uncomfortable in my own skin.

Christmas arrived, yet thoughts of those stolen toys elbowed their way between me and the Christmas spirit. I had to do something to ease this discomfort. But what? Ideally, I should have returned to the Pine Cone Gift Shop and just paid for the items, but I didn't have the courage to do that. I justified my indecisive weakness by telling myself that it was winter and our family was too far away from Promised Land for me to make restitution.

One Saturday night, I came up with a solution.

"Tomorrow we're going to church," I reminded myself. "What if I put the money I should have used to pay for the Yo-yos into the collection plate? That would square my account with both the gift shop and God and help rid me of this guilty conscience." I'm not sure that's exactly how I thought things through. All I remember is that the logic seemed sound.

The next morning, before church, I raided my piggy bank (yes, I had one) and reluctantly pulled out $30 from the allowance I had been saving. Then, in church, after the hymns and the scripture readings were done, the offering plate was passed. When it reached my pew, I reached into my pocket, pulled out my payment, and, while hiding my "contribution" from my mother, yet fighting the urge to hang onto my cash, I forced my hand to drop it into the plate, and away it went, carrying my guilt with it. I felt good. I had paid my dues. The account was cleared. And then, the preacher began his sermon.

"Friends, God wants us to know, through his word, that we cannot buy our way into Heaven."

My face sank. I was horrified. Yes, the sermon was based on the Bible verse that says it's easier for a camel to go through the eye of a needle than for a rich man to enter the Kingdom of God. I had made my situation worse. Not only had my guilt returned, now I was going to Hell.

Over the years, I would occasionally think of what I had lost by stealing 14 Yo-yos. The ache of my guilt dissipated with time, of course, but would suddenly flare up, like the pain of an old wound. But there was nothing I could do to salve it.

When I was in my mid-thirties, I returned to Promised Land with my wife, Mary; our two children, Bethany and Ian; and friends we had made while stationed with the Army in Germany. The cottage we rented was less than a half mile from the Pine Cone Gift Shop. I decided to take a walk.

"Hi, my name's Tony Nauroth, and I'm here to pay an old debt," I told the young woman behind the counter.

Stunned, she asked, "What do you mean?"

"Well, I'm embarrassed to tell you this, but a long time ago I came in here and shoplifted 14 yo-yos ..."

"Fourteen!" she marveled. "Why did you need 14 yo-yos?"

That was a very good question, but I had no answer.

"I don't know," I said.

"Well, why are you here today?"

"I'd like to pay for them. I've had a guilty conscience for years, and I can't stand it anymore."

She burst out laughing, then said, "Oh, honey. The people who owned this place back then are long gone. You don't have to pay me anything. Keep your money."

Flabbergasted, I said, "Now what do I do? Are you sure you don't want the money? I should have paid $30 for them."

"No, you keep your money. That's all right. You just coming in to tell me this is payment enough."

"But I have to do something," I objected.

"Well, how about if you donate it to your church?"

Now it was my turn to be stunned. "I tried that," I said. "It didn't work."

"Well, what can I do to help? I can forgive you. I can do that."

"You would?"

"Yes, you seem like a good guy. So I forgive you."

Maybe that was enough. I thanked her, stuffed my money back into my pocket, and walked out, being careful to avoid the toy aisle and thinking to myself, "Sometimes you just can't make this stuff up," and wondering what fate all those Yo-yos endured.

*   *   *

(Tony, Confucius tells us that "A man who has committed a mistake and doesn't correct it, is committing another mistake." It seems you have merely one strike against you, if we are keeping score. Still, walking the dog out of a store without paying for it can also land you in the Dog House ... or some other type of confinement.

I don't think I have any memories of crimes I have committed. I mostly collect "fun-times-and-places memories" and get to re-visit them every time I come across one of the many bags that are folded and stacked neatly in a pile that just keeps growing and growing and growing. What can I say ... lucky me ... to have too many happy times. – Becky)

CHAPTER 14

Storing Memories in Store Bags

Becky

*"A writer is like a bag lady going through life
with a sack and a pointed stick collecting stuff."*

– Tony Hillerman
(*Author of detective novels*)

Daniel Storto's Glove Museum remembered.

I have always liked history, and I love to travel, so living in Germany from June 1986 to 1991 gave us a chance to live through a little piece of history that took place in Europe during that time.

When we arrived in Nuremberg, the Berlin Wall – that 27-mile stretch of concrete and barbed wire constructed by the East Germans in August of 1961 to separate East and West Berlin – was standing and being patrolled by armed guards. With special papers from the military, we were allowed to travel by train to visit both East and West Berlin.

The West was like any other western vibrant city. The East was so very different. It was gray and stark. The stores offered few choices, and although I did buy yarn and a few down comforters, they were not the quality we found in the western parts of Germany. The upside was that things were inexpensive, so we shopped. We went to East Berlin several times. It was important to show our 10- and 11-year-olds the difference between a free capitalistic society and life under communism. The contrast was stunning. I think they noticed the difference right away, especially in foods!

We were there when the Berlin Wall came down on Nov. 9, 1989. I have an actual piece of that history! It is a tiny piece of the wall. The world then witnessed a truly world-shaking event on October 3, 1990 with the reunification of East and West Germany.

We visited the city of Prague in Czechoslovakia in 1987, before it had opened to the West. It was a city rich in history buried under soot and many years of neglect. When we returned to Prague (now in the Czech Republic) after 1990, we were absolutely mesmerized by the breathtaking beauty of the newly restored Golden City. Tourists came from around the world to enjoy this vibrant place. We went there often.

Ralph and I were strolling through the city's Old Town Square late one night. It was magical to be there during the time of such historic change. In the darkness of the evening, we heard a familiar voice singing on the other side of the courtyard. We walked over and saw a figure of a man sitting on a stage that had been constructed for some sort of concert. It was the famous Richie Havens, who was so much a part of Woodstock and the young generation of the 1960s. He was sitting alone and singing, probably checking the sound system that had been set up. He pointed to a small flier that announced an event called the "FREEDOM CONCERT" that would take place the very next day.

We went to that concert and stood shoulder to shoulder in the packed crowd to watch the show. It was like "Woodstock in Prague" for us! Joe Cocker, Richie Havens, and Billy Preston sang to an unbelievably enthusiastic audience from all over the world! No one wanted the concert to end. I still have that little Handwritten Flier announcing the concert. It is among the Stuff I cannot part with and have kept for 33 years. And even now I can hear the unmistakable voice of Richie Havens singing his song "Freedom" every time I see it.

Returning home and unpacking my suitcase after every vacation, I would end up with bags from museums and shops. Bags with the shop names and addresses, in foreign languages emblazoned on the front, allowed me to relive the memorable times in so many interesting places that we had visited.

In London, we saw the musicals "Les Miserables" with the original cast, and "Miss Saigon" too. I bought sweatshirts from both and still have the bags. The shirts are worn thin, but the bags are fine. I bought a canister of tea in the world-famous Harrods of London. It came in a bag. Hilo Hatties was a landmark in Honolulu. It had the largest inventory of Hawaiian Stuff, and I picked up more than a few souvenirs there during the four years we lived on that island. Those bags are covered with images of huge hibiscus, the Hawaiian state flower.

When Ralph retired from the military after 29+ years, we continued the adventure of living overseas. He accepted a contract position in Vicenza, Italy where we happily lived for six years, and I happily collected "high-end" bags from factory outlets like Armani, Bottega Veneta, Fratelli Rossetti, etc.

In August 2008, we finally settled down in Easton, Pennsylvania, and I unpacked a lifetime of stuff, including, by then, my enormous bag collection. I folded them flat and dropped them into a basket near the front door. My intention was to grab a bag and use it to carry purchases home. Unfortunately, those bags were filled with memories and too nice to use.

Easton is an hour's drive from New York City and that fun-filled destination became our new stomping ground. The opera, ballet, museums, and Broadway filled us with such thrilling memories and added quickly to my collection. I soon accumulated a seemingly bottomless pile of memories in a bottomless pile of bags! The tiniest bag in the collection is from a fascinating visit to Daniel Storto's Glove Museum in Dorloo, New York.

At an art show, while visiting our son in Massachusetts, I saw an interesting tote bag. It was crocheted using plastic bags that had been torn into strips and used as yarn. The vendor said it was a perfect way to recycle plastic bags. She gave me instructions, and it seemed like a very good idea until I stood staring at my collection with scissors in hand. It was hopeless.

It seems to me that the stuff we find so difficult to part with is the very stuff we are supposed to keep. I just need to be more selective about the bags I carry home, because that is where they will remain forever.

*　*　*

(Becky, I too remember those shopping trips to East Berlin. Once I bought a three-piece suit for $17.50! I no longer have it, and even if I did, it would never fit me anymore. And I no longer have the bag it came in. I can see that you're out of control, turning bags into baggage, but at least it's emotional baggage! If collecting them makes you feel that good – especially when they remind you of a memorable person, a happy place, or a beautiful thing – then why not? Maybe I should have kept one of my most precious items of stuff in one of your bags. Then I would know where to find it – your house! – Tony)

CHAPTER 15

Uncle Ben's Ring

Tony

*"Things we lose have a way of coming back to us in the end,
if not always in the way we expect."*

*– J.K. Rowling
(British author, "Harry Potter")*

Tony with his Uncle Ben in Harrisburg, 1952.

*U*ncle Ben Linkus sits in his Barca-lounger in the living room of his home on Emerald Street in Harrisburg, Pennsylvania. His wife, Aunt Fracie, is in the kitchen with my mother, Betty Nauroth, and Jean Daugherty. Jean is my aunt; Fracie is my mother's aunt. For part of her life, Betty lived with Fracie and Ben. They have always been close.

Aunt Fracie is a lovely woman, tall and straight in both physical and moral stature. She chatters in a voice that approaches a screech, although inexplicably pleasant, and she darts around her kitchen in quick moves. I am reminded of a mama bird flitting around her nest, keeping her nestlings comfortable and their bellies full.

Uncle Ben fascinates me. A round man with a white mustache and shock of pure white hair, he is the perfect picture of a Civil War era southern gentleman, made more so by the pure white suits he always wore, topped with a black string tie around his neck, like the exclamation point at the end of a South Carolina drawl. Uncle Ben had that drawl. He was born somewhere in the South. Years later, I would be astonished to discover his twin in the Kentucky Fried Chicken television commercials. The first time I noticed the resemblance and asked him if he owned a food company, he chuckled and drawled, "If I did, Tony, I wouldn't be living this far north. I'd own a plantation in Mississippi." He pronounced the state's name as if it were located on a different planet. Like I said, he fascinated me.

Uncle Ben wore a heavy gold ring on his right hand. It had a flat face with the initials H.B.L. engraved on it. Sometimes I would finger the ring and rub my little digits over its carvings. Sometimes he would even take it off and let me hold it.

"Uncle Ben," I asked one day, "What do these letters mean?"

"That's my name, Tony."

"HBL? That's a strange name." (I pronounced out the letters as "Hubble.")

He laughed and said, "No, those are my initials. The H is for Herbert, the L stands for Linkus, my last name, and the big one in the middle – the B – is for my middle name, Ben."

"Oh!" I exclaimed, "Like Benjamin Franklin."

He corrected my slightly askew moment of discovery, saying, "No, Tony, just Ben, not Benjamin."

"Oh, okay." That's like my middle name – just Ben."

"Yes, exactly. Your mommy gave you your middle name from me."

"Wow! I didn't know that," I said.

"I'll tell you what, Tony. When you get old enough, I'm going to give this ring to you. Then you can wear it and remember me."

"That'd be great, Uncle Ben. Thank you! I can hardly wait!"

He laughed and said, "Well, I'm not ready to go just yet."

My family visited Ben and Fracie frequently. We usually stayed at Aunt Jean's house where my five siblings and I enjoyed the company of my cousins, Tim and Dave Daugherty. They didn't have a southern accent. Their father, Ammon Daugherty (We always knew him as Uncle Doc) was a favorite of ours. Always telling jokes and filled with good humor, he kept us entertained and we were always excited to visit him, although during baseball season, if the Philadelphia Phillies were losing, he got a little grumpy. He was a great baseball fan.

One day, he told us that he had something special planned.

"Kids, how would you like to go for a train ride?"

"Yeah!" and "Yay!" we all screamed.

"Tomorrow," he said, "we'll get on a train and go to Philadelphia, to Connie Mack Stadium for a baseball game."

"On TV?" my younger brother David asked.

Laughing, Uncle Doc said, "No, we'll be there right in the stands, and we'll have hot dogs and popcorn, and we'll have a lot of fun."

Uncle Doc Daugherty worked for the railroad, so we traveled by train to the City of Brotherly Love for free. I wasn't particularly interested in the game, I just wanted to get back on the train to feel it sway, listen to the clickety-clack of the rails, and watch the countryside roll by; to move. I remember that trip with fondness, joy, and sadness.

A few days later, after we had returned to our home near Wilkes-Barre, we learned that Uncle Ben had passed away; died in his Barca-lounger, in his white suit and black string tie. Gone back South, it seemed. We returned to Harrisburg to attend the funeral, then to Aunt Fracie's house for a funeral dinner. No one sat in the Barca-lounger.

When we left, Aunt Fracie pulled me aside and put a small black box into my hand.

"Your Uncle Ben wanted you to have this, Sweetie," she said.

I knew what it was. The ring. The ring he had promised me. He actually came through. I felt a huge emotional bubble rise into my chest, and it burst through in heaving sobs.

I kept that ring for a long while before I wore it. Part of me simply couldn't break away from the thought that this was Uncle Ben's ring, not Tony Ben's ring. A ring like that would bear the initials A.B.N., not H.B.L. But we did share that "B", and one day, after my fingers had grown some, I slipped it on, and it stayed. I never took it off again.

As I aged, my fingers seemed to shrink a bit. Instead of gripping my right ring finger tightly, the gold band began to move, but it still held on, although I was planning to get it resized.

During the spring of 2023, decades after Uncle Ben, Aunt Fracie, Uncle Doc, Aunt Jean, and even Tim and David had passed on, I was out in our yard cleaning up winter's debris. Our tall trees had shed sticks now scattered across the lawn, and the garden was full of weeds that had to be pulled. It was a long day of hard work, grasping and tossing nature's annual detritus – the stuff of plant life, and death – into barrels and boxes.

When I came inside to wash up, I could sense that something was wrong, but I couldn't quite put my finger on it. Then, when I absentmindedly went to fiddle with Uncle Ben's ring – as I often did – I discovered only flesh, no gold. In a panic, I tried to remember what I had done with it, but I put the obvious answer out of my mind – somewhere in the yard. Somewhere.

I frantically ran outside and walked the lawn in a grid pattern, like an archaeologist searching an ancient dig site. When I finished, I was a frustrated and disappointed digger.

I glanced over at the four-foot-high pile of sticks stacked against the trunk of the maple tree out front, ready for town employees to pick it up and cart it off to the compost center. I took a chair and a large barrel over to that pile, sat down, and painstakingly sifted through small handfuls of twigs, discarding much of it into the barrel. For three hours I worked, and only when I got to the point where a thin layer of leaves remained on the ground did I know the ring was not there.

I sat there a few moments, crestfallen, and so very disappointed in my carelessness. That ring was special to me. Not just a dew-drop jewel to strike the fancy of others; not just stuff wrapped around my finger. I stared at the pale ring now exposed on my skin where the object of my affection had rested. I felt naked. This was an heirloom, something that I had planned to give to my son, Ian, after his finger grew into it.

Then I remembered that among the many chores I took care of this day, I had refilled the big bucket of birdseed out back. I mix regular seeds with sunflower seeds to draw different avian species to our yard. In so doing I use my right hand as a one-tool scoop and mixer. Perhaps I had lost the ring in there. I wouldn't have even felt it leave me.

Picking up my chair, I ran to the bucket, found another bucket, sat down, removed the lids, and pulled handful after handful of seed out, letting it dribble ever so slowly through my fingers into the empty container. Another two hours passed, and when I got to the last smidgen of seeds, I knew the ring was gone – really gone.

I gave up.

That night, I barely slept.

"Where could it be? Where could it be?" I asked myself, over and over. Every once in a while, I would jump up and scurry to a place where I just knew it had to be. Once I ran to check where I had been doing laundry earlier that day; once where I had been working at my workbench in the basement; once when I thought I might have taken it off while playing my guitar. But I never take it off when I play.

The next day, tired and miserable, I told my wife Mary how horrible I felt, and asked her if she had any ideas. She didn't, but she commiserated with me, and grew sad for me, which made me feel better.

A few days later, Mary handed me a little black box, just like Aunt Fracie had once done. Inside was a ring! But it wasn't THE ring. This one was gold, like Uncle Ben's, but instead of initials engraved on top, an oval garnet stone shone darkly from its mounting.

"This is to replace your ring," Mary said.

I was touched by her thoughtfulness and placed it on my finger. It was a bit large, and right away I worried that I might lose it also.

"Maybe I'll get it resized," I thought, this time really meaning it.

It's been quite a while since I lost Uncle Ben's ring, and I'm still wearing Mary's garnet one. It's not a replacement ring, it's a "place-holder ring," which is what Mary now calls it. This ring is there but for the moment when I inadvertently stumble across a flash of gold somewhere I had not checked before. The original ring hasn't really disappeared; it's just waiting to be rediscovered.

I often think of those Harrisburg visits, and the last image I have of Aunt Fracie is her smiling and waving goodbye from her front porch. I even have a picture of her leaning against the porch post, which no longer exists. Her home on Emerald Street (I wish it had been named Garnet Street) is now an empty lot, strewn with the stuff of a house torn down long ago, where I'd like to think Uncle Ben's ghost still haunts his Barca-lounger. Perhaps this is what happened to my prize. Perhaps both he and his H.B.L. ring have gone South.

* * *

(Tony! I think that ring will appear one day. It may have fallen somewhere inside your house, under the seat in your car, or maybe it had slipped off when you were reaching into a drawer for something. It could have slipped off anywhere and you may have just noticed it at the end of a long day of yard work. That is my hope. In the meantime, as you frantically searched for his ring, your memories of Uncle Ben and his impact on your life must have become even more intense. And then, Mary stepped in to show how much she feels your sadness, and that must warm your heart. So, in the end, maybe tangible things that disappear are replaced with thoughts and emotions that linger in our hearts. Your story also made me think of my lost ring. – Becky)

CHAPTER 16

A Puzzling Vanishing Act

Becky

*"There are three rings involved with marriage:
The engagement ring, the wedding ring, and the suffering."*

– *Woody Allen*
(American humorist and filmmaker)

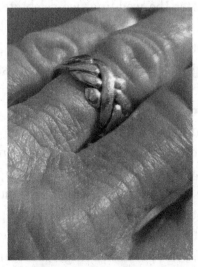

Amazing puzzle ring.

*I*n anticipation of our wedding ceremony, planned to take place in the home of my parents, Ralph and I found ourselves at a jewelry counter staring at an ocean of sparkling rings. I wanted just a simple thin gold band, but here under the bright lights, a rather unusual and much larger and expensive ring caught my eye. It shimmered, shiny and buffed gold, in a pattern that reminded me of long petals of a daisy marching upright around my finger.

"Can I see that one?" I asked the lady patiently waiting on the other side of the counter. I pointed to the set.

"Which one?" Ralph asked, squinting into the display case. "Do you mean the one that looks sort of like a standing rib roast?"

"Yes" I said. "they're perfect."

We made the purchase and tucked them away to await the wedding day. Then, during the ceremony, we slipped those rings onto each other's fingers where they would stay – happily and forever after.

That 'happily forever after' part was not quite the prediction made by friends, and even some of our family members. We certainly thought we would stay together forever, but statistics said we were much too young to make long-lasting decisions like choosing a life-long soulmate. Statistics could even predict how long the marriage would last.

A few weeks after the wedding, we celebrated with a party at my parents' home where we lived on the floor below them until Ralph finished dental school. At almost midnight, as our guests were leaving and getting into their cars, Ralph and I stood on the front lawn waving goodbye. It was a great celebratory evening with close friends, and we were giddy with happiness.

Just for fun, Ralph picked me up, sweeping me off my feet while I extended my arm over my head in a big waving motion. It was perfectly choreographed, and I felt like an Olympian on ice at the end of a dramatic skating routine. At that very moment, as I glided through the air, I felt my golden wedding band glide right off my finger and up into the air as I swirled around under the stars! When I returned to earth, I saw my naked finger and frantically yelled.

"My wedding ring! It's gone!"

Friends returned from their cars to help search in the dark, but I sent them home saying I would find it in the morning.

I woke up and combed through the grass in search of that ring and never stopped looking for it. Metal detectors showed up in the arms of friends and ladders to check the roof were dragged into the yard. I even carried a magnifying glass to check each blade of grass and the mulch and dirt in the garden. Nothing has ever been so GONE. It just vanished.

I remember the day we left Washington, D.C. to drive to Lamar, Colorado with everything we owned tied to the top of my 1966 Rambler (See Chapter 18: "The Turquoise Rambler American"). Ralph was taking part in a University of Colorado Health Services program for migrant workers in that area. He would do dentistry for the summer, and then we would drive straight to Fort Sam Houston for Officer's Basic Training Course. In September, when the program was completed, he would report to his first duty station in Stuttgart, Germany. We were leaving home forever.

As we pulled away from my parents' house and waved goodbye to my mom and my brother standing at the door, I thought of that wedding band hiding somewhere, never to be recovered. The house was sold many years ago. I wondered if it was a very bad omen that we threw that wedding band away. I worried our marriage too might be only a bright fleeting shiny moment in our lives; but after more than 57 years together, I have put superstition and that thought to rest.

We replaced the lost ring with a thin gold band we purchased at the PX (Post Exchange store) the day Ralph entered the military. Then, a few years later, on a trip to Greece, I fell in love with a gold 'puzzle ring' that can be taken apart, forming a long chain. It was difficult to rebuild. It took time and patience, but eventually the ring could be restored. I think this puzzle ring is quite appropriate – a symbol of our marriage. It does seem, at times, the most intricate puzzle of all.

* * *

(*Becky, it seems we've both learned that yard work and acrobatics are not kind to loose-fitting jewelry! But isn't it strange that when we replace what was lost, the replacement eventually becomes the stuff we cherish, as if there was no loss at all? At least that's the way it's been with me.*

I am reminded of yet another ring I lost years ago when I was stationed at Fort Devens, Massachusetts. Coincidentally, it also involved acrobatics. My platoon was undergoing physical training, and at the time, one of the required exercises was negotiating hand-over-hand monkey bars. To prevent my wedding band from cutting into my finger, I took it off and set it to the side. It's probably still there. We replaced it with something a little fancier, with an engraved geometric design and three diamond chips. It's pretty cool!

Speaking of cool, did I ever tell you about my great grandfather's dairy and the old "Nauroth" milk bottle I tracked down? And do you even remember milk bottles and milkmen? Read on and enjoy! – Tony)

CHAPTER 17

History All Bottled Up

Tony

*"You spend the first part of your life collecting things
and the second half getting rid of them."*

*– Isabel Allende
(Chilean author, "House of the Spirits")*

A "Nauroth Dairy" milk bottle.

$\mathcal{L}$ ong ago, someone in Allentown, Pennsylvania went out their front door to pick up the bottle of fresh milk left there by the milkman. It was a time when there were such things as milkmen, back when milk was delivered, not in paper, but in bottles, like the one I now lovingly held swaddled in my hands.

Molded right into the glass, barely visible until I hold it up to the light just so, are the words, "Nauroth Dairy" along with the dairy's Gordon Street address, near Second Street in Allentown.

More than 100 years ago, my great-grandfather, August Nauroth, opened Nauroth's Dairy and established his milk routes using horse-drawn wagons. I knew my family had been in the dairy business, but I never knew the details and never asked about it until a few years ago. I heard stories about how one of August's relatives absconded with a huge amount of cash milked from the family business and fled to Texas, but that might be more myth than memory.

I was doing some family research when I ran across an Internet connection to the dairy. The reference was thin, but it included a photograph of an old Nauroth Dairy milk bottle. I thought that would be a wonderful link with the past to display somewhere in our house. But even if I did find one, it would probably be very expensive, so I satisfied myself by printing the picture and pasting it into my journal.

A few days later, the "Penny Power," our local shopper newspaper, arrived on my doorstep. I perused the ads – mostly looking for yard sales, which I normally do – when my eye fell on an item announcing the 26th Annual Bux-Mont Bottle Show (Bux-Mont is the local shorthand for Bucks and Montgomery counties in Southeastern Pennsylvania). I instantly thought, "Hey, I might be able to find a Nauroth milk bottle there." I didn't even know some people collected bottles. Apparently, any stuff can be collected.

My wife Mary and I drove to the Tylersport Fire Company on April 2, 2023. We were in no hurry. We learned from the ad that they were charging early arrivals $10 to get in, and $3 after 9 a.m. I supposed the early bird fee was in place to entice true early-bird collectors who might otherwise miss out on the best worms or, in this case, bottles.

Mary stayed in the car. It didn't make sense for us to spend $6 just to check a few bottles. I told her I would be right back. But when I paid my fee and walked in, I was confronted with scores of tables groaning under the glass weight of thousands upon thousands of bottles that once held myriads of stuff – perfume and pickles, ointments and oregano, jelly jars and Jamaican rum, mothballs and yes, milk.

"I'll be here for hours," I thought with dismay. I even considered abandoning my quest. But I was here; might as well have a quick look-see.

I began inching my way down the first aisle, slowly studying the varied sizes and shapes glimmering in the morning sunshine. Three tables and twenty minutes later, I realized this was too inefficient. I decided to simply ask the vendors if they had any "Nauroth Dairy" milk bottles. Their answers were always, "No, sorry." I began to lose hope of finding my imagined treasure and was ready to quit.

"One more aisle," I said to myself, and I pushed on.

When I got about halfway through the second row of tables, I asked a vendor, "Do you happen to have a milk bottle from Nauroth's Dairy? It used to be in Allentown."

"No, sorry, I don't."

But a man standing in the aisle turned to me and said, "I have one."

"Really?" I exclaimed.

"Yes, but I don't have it with me today."

He said his name was David Long. He was a collector and also a vendor at this day's event. I must have looked disappointed, but he said, "I could get it to you tomorrow, though."

I brightened and asked, "How much do you want for it?"

"Fifteen dollars." As far as I was concerned, he was giving it to me. We made arrangements for me to pick up the bottle at his home near Lake Nockamixon the next day.

"I won't be home," David said. "Just pull in the driveway. It'll be in front of my garage – in the milk box."

How appropriate.

"Do I pay you now?"

"Just leave the money in the milk box."

Special delivery, I supposed.

The next morning, Mary and I drove to the lake, found David's home, and pulled into the driveway. I went over to the milk box – a square aluminum container with a lid that raises on a hinge – peered in, and there was my prize, just as promised. It was a little dirty, but it was real, and when I touched it I immediately felt a thrilling connection to my past. I dropped $20 into the milk box and closed the lid.

A few days later, Mary and I drove to the Gordon Street address that was embossed on the bottle. The dairy building was still there, now turned into apartments, with a Pentecostal Church occupying one end. I took photos of the building, which I also pasted into my journal, next to the one from the Internet and a new one of my bottle. The actual bottle holds a place of honor on the top center of our beautiful dining room hutch.

Decades after August Nauroth founded his dairy, it – along with several other family-owned dairies – was sold and folded into the newly established Lehigh Valley Dairy, Inc. Milkmen, along with milk bottles, disappeared.

On the one hand, I do realize that my bottle is merely a breakable piece of glass stuff. On the other hand, where it used to hold milk it now holds memories, and I am terrified that it might fall off the hutch and break. More likely, though, it will eventually end up being sold at a bottle show.

* * *

(Tony, what a sweet visit into your past. I miss our milkman. That fresh milk left on our doorstep was above and beyond what we drink today. I'm sure I was not the only child to take the cream off the top to make butter. Ending up with less than a thimbleful did not fulfill my expectations. I also discovered my family was not fond of skim milk. Thank you for reminding me of those special mornings

opening that silver metal box to get those bottles of creamy sweet milk, sealed with a disk of waxy cardboard and a foil cap on top. I can feel it clenched tightly in my chubby little hands as I carefully walk it into the kitchen … much like how I clutch tightly to those joyous memories of mornings long gone.

Speaking of nostalgia … as a young adult it was very difficult to let go of my first car. – Becky)

CHAPTER 18

The Turquoise Rambler American

Becky

"Roads were made for journeys, not destinations."

– Confucius
  (Fifth century B.C.E. philosopher)

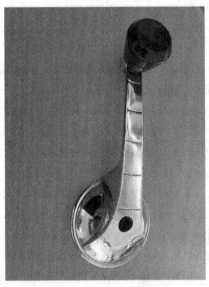

Vintage Turquoise Rambler crank.

*I*t was September of 1973, and Ralph and I and 5-year-old Scott were heading to Stuttgart, Germany. It was Ralph's first duty station after signing up with the U.S. Army and then graduating from dental school. We had just spent the entire summer in Lamar, Colorado where Ralph was part of a Health Services program sponsored by the University of Colorado to provide dental care to migrant workers in that area. Right after his graduation, we packed my beloved Turquoise Rambler American (my very first car) with everything we owned, including Scott's bike, and drove straight out to Colorado. We marveled at the enormous never-ending sky.

We spent the summer in a tiny stucco house. Scott discovered that if he dropped a marble at the back door it rolled out the front in exactly 17 seconds. There were 7,000 people in Lamar. It was the hottest summer on record with the temperature hovering around 107 degrees. We watched the Watergate Hearings on a tiny TV we brought with us. We had an antenna made of every piece of wire we could find.

Scott and I would spend some afternoons at the big community pool where we met all the children of the migrant workers who attended swimming classes there. At home, I kept Scott and the two neighbor children busy with art projects. With bags of flour, string, and jars of brightly colored day-glow paints, we made paper-mache beaded curtains for our house. Then we made brightly decorated bracelets and gave them to the migrant children.

In August, we packed up my Rambler American once again and headed for Fort Sam Houston in San Antonio, Texas. We lived in a tiny motel room across from a children's amusement park. Scott wanted to live there forever. Ralph had six weeks of Officer's Basic Training before entering the Army Dental Corps. He learned how to put on his uniform and insignia, how to salute, and march, and much more about life in the Army. The plan was to serve for a few years, pay off student loans, save some money, open a dental practice somewhere, and live happily ever after.

Six weeks later we were on our way back to D.C. to pack up any belongings we had and to ship them off to Stuttgart. That included my little Rambler American. How lucky we were to be going to Europe!

We were met at Frankfurt International Airport by our sponsor, Harry Sunshine (his real name), who drove us straight to the Essinger farmhouse. Dr. Sunshine had arranged for us to rent the little house that had previously been rented to the Army dentist Ralph was replacing. Harry introduced us to the Essinger family – Herr and Frau Essinger, their 16-year-old daughter, and their 9-year-old son.

Frau Essinger showed us around the two-story apartment, which was attached to their home. It was nice but had sand-blasted walls the color of sand and looked very bland and a little sad to me. Shortly after moving in, we painted the two WCs (water closets, which are rooms with only a toilet) all in bright royal blue and fire-engine red shiny enamel paint. We had gigantic arrows in different colors for each wall pointing downward from the ceiling and alternated the colors to have a dramatic effect. When you opened the door to use the restroom it was anything but restful. We did the hallway in canary yellow, but brighter than any canary I had ever seen.

We were so excited about decorating, we never thought that there was a good possibility that enamel paint would be impossible to remove from sand-blasted walls. All I know is that the Essingers were VERY surprised to see the new look we had given the formerly sedate premises. I vividly remember running over to get them to show them what we had done; and they came into the house and, with eyes very wide, looked and said, "Ohhhh! Look what you've done!!" But in German it had a more guttural ACHHHH sound. But they liked it, I think. They kept looking at each other and then back at the walls.

"Oh, don't worry," I said. "We will paint it back the way it was."

But Frau Essinger, in her cheerful way, said in German, "No no no, don't even think of it."

It was many years later, when I got a little smarter, that it occurred to me there was no way to get those walls back to the way they were, except to sand-blast them again. That can't be an inexpensive way to finish off walls.

We had such fun living there. Frau Essinger would come to my kitchen window every evening when she was finishing chores, and we would talk and she would watch me cook. She knew no English and she was speaking a dialect, unlike the German I was learning in my University of Maryland courses. But language was not that important; we understood each other very well. I adored her.

They thought everything we did was funny. We invited them over and they were shocked to see our waterbed that took up most of the living room. We dared not put it upstairs. When we had them over for a barbecue, I served corn on the cob, which in Germany was only used as feed for animals. We laughed a lot.

The day after our arrival Ralph bought a car, a brand-new Volvo Station Wagon. It was British racing green with a chocolate brown leather interior. Why he would buy a Volvo station wagon to go camping around Europe escapes me, but that is exactly what he did.

Then, we got the news that my car – the turquoise 1966 Rambler American – was waiting for us at the dock in Bremerhaven, Germany. I loved that car and could not wait to pick it up! We had driven it across the country several times during dental school years; then out to Lamar with everything we owned tied onto the top, stuffed into the interior, and hanging out of the windows. Then it transported us to Texas and into the Army. And now, it had crossed the ocean to be part of our European adventure.

We arrived at the dock lot at Bremerhaven, near the North Sea, and spotted the Rambler right away. It looked so beautiful sitting there in the ocean of cars – so blue and so American; so very American. This was the car that I decorated with Flower Power stickers for years when it was new. And, with my first paycheck, I bought Scott a small metal turquoise peddle car that looked exactly like mine. He would park it on the grass and we would wash our cars together every Sunday afternoon.

We walked into the office, took care of the paperwork, jumped in the car, and headed for the exit. At the first stop sign, we stalled, and it took a few tries to get it started again. Then we drove a little bit farther and came to another stop sign, stalled again, and had to wait and keep trying to start it until finally we were off again. It happened again, and we decided to not stop at all for the entire trip to Stuttgart because we were so afraid it might not start up again. We sort of knew there was something really wrong with the car, but we figured we had to make it home because we had no other choice. So at every traffic light, we slowed down and coasted until the light turned green and then we floored it. As soon as we pulled up in front of the Essingers' farmhouse, my car fizzled out and we needed to tow it to a garage the next day to get it fixed.

Next, we had to get the Rambler inspected. The Germans are very serious about their inspections. The first time we brought it over, it did not pass. There were several little problems, one being that there was a little hole in the floor in front of the back seat. It needed some sheet metal welded to the rusted bottom of the car so we could drive it. No one wanted to weld it because it was too close to the gas tank. Ralph took some tin foil and installed layers and layers of black undercoating and came up with a pretty thick layer of protection. We thought maybe this would work. I decided to wait until the day before Christmas to drive it over to the inspection station thinking maybe everyone would be in a hurry to get home. It passed! We then had time to look for a real professional who did the welding and kept it running and passing every inspection for the next three years.

At the end of Ralph's tour of duty, it was sad to pack up our things to leave Germany. We enjoyed living there, and we did a lot of traveling too. We did not purchase much because the dollar made a swift downward slide on the day of our arrival in Germany, so everything was expensive. With the dollar at an all-time low, we were pretty much leaving with exactly the same stuff we had brought over with us. Well, we did have one additional item – nine-month-old Jason.

It was an exciting time because the next duty station would be Fort Clayton, Panama City, Panama. Now that I had "mastered" an extremely flawed and incomprehensible German, I was ready to sink my teeth into the Spanish language and see what damage I could do.

I was heartbroken that my dear old Rambler American would not make this move with us. I hoped to find an American who would love it and who could keep it running. The perfect young soldier appeared and couldn't wait to get my car! I told him to come on Thursday, the day after the movers would pick up all our stuff.

The big moving van packed up our waterbed, two bright red bean bag chairs, 12 wooden crates painted with red and royal blue enamel paint, a bright red picnic table, two boxes of kitchen things, a few boxes of clothes, and three bikes. Oh, and some record albums and books were also tossed on the truck.

It's always a great feeling when the last item is shoved into the van and I sit staring at the emptiness of the home I'm leaving. There is a part of me that truly does not care if our moving container were to fall off the ship in the middle of the Atlantic Ocean. The lightness of having only a packed suitcase is refreshing. I am not sure how long that feeling lasts. Probably just a few weeks. I just thought of how nice it would be to get home after a long vacation and see all our stuff!

The next day at noon the doorbell rang, and the young soldier introduced himself and said he absolutely loved the car sitting outside our front door. He told us he likes to work on cars, and he would get this running like new, and how much he really appreciated that we would sell it to him for a dollar. I don't think I have ever seen anyone that happy. We walked out to the car and stood there talking with the blistering August sun beating down on us. Finally, we said goodbye, and he thanked us again and again before getting into that Beautiful Blue Rambler American shining in the hot sun! He sat gripping the steering wheel and looked up at us through the side window with a big proud smile across his face. Then he looked down for a moment, then looked back up at us through the window, and then looked back down.

It was very hot and that poor soldier had sweat pouring down into his eyes and falling off his cheeks, which were turning a bright crimson. Finally, he opened the door, leaned out, and said, "Excuse me, but how do I open the windows?"

I looked at him in complete silence for a moment. He opened the door a little wider and asked, "Where are the window cranks?"

I stared back pondering the question, and then in a very sad and melancholy voice said, "Oh, they are in my jewelry box. I wanted to keep the window cranks to remind me of all the good times we shared with this car. Oh dear, they were shipped yesterday."

He smiled weakly and said he could probably use a wrench or pliers.

"I'm afraid the movers shipped everything," I said.

With a small sigh, he started the engine and slowly left the Essinger driveway, still clutching the open door.

I still have and treasure those cranks, although I do feel a little guilty when I look at them.

*   *   *

(Becky, those troubles with your favorite car – despite being troubling – are pretty funny. Now I'm thinking about all the cars I ever had and wondering if I have any window cranks, floor mats, hubcaps, or other pieces from any of them. I don't, but I do have their memories. Be prepared for a journey through the automobile industry and my connection to each brand. Read on! – Tony)

CHAPTER 19

A Cavalcade of Cars

Tony

"Whatever you have, you must either use, or lose."

– Henry Ford
(Pioneering U.S. Auto manufacturer)

Tony's mother, brother, and the 1950s family car.

*T*he automobile, to me, is merely the means to a road trip, while road trips are the real stuff of life. Cars are how we get from point A to point B, and are the means to experience everything in between – from point C to point Z. When I hear a guy waxing eloquent about his Corvette convertible with dual carburetors, glass-pack exhausts, and extra doohickeys jammed under the hood; or when I hear a teenage testosterone-injected high school senior rumble out from the school parking lot across the street from my home, I shake my head and mutter, "Jeeze, it's only a car."

I don't own a collection of cars, not stuff on wheels. But I do possess a collection of memories from the time I did own each of my cars. It's almost as if I've been collecting the souls of those cars; gathering ghosts from the machines that are just as real as the metal, leather, glass, and rubber that once embodied those spirits.

Memories like this one:

My wife Mary and I used to share our home with a black and tan coon hound named Sadie. She loved road trips (Sadie, not Mary, who doesn't care for them all that much). A medium-sized dog with an oversized ambition, Sadie would leap into our little Honda Civic and run around in circles in the back seat like she didn't have a brain in her head. But once the car started, she settled next to the rolled down window, and away we went – her ears and tongue flapping in the breeze, and a big smile on her face. When we got to where we were going, she grew forlorn and impatient, and the smile on her snout turned into a frown as if she were saying, "Well, let's go!"

The cars of our past do bring up such fond recollections. And, when I think of all those that have sped through my life, I too am tempted to wax eloquent. Following are just some of the ghosts that travel with me on this road trip of life.

THE KAISER:

In the mid-1950s, my father had a pale blue Kaiser, a big, heavy, roundish behemoth. The brand went the way of the dodo long ago. It sat in our backyard, except when it was in use. The strange thing is that I don't remember ever riding in it, but I must have. Then again, I was probably only three or four years old.

BETSY:

We called her – and she was a her – Betsy. She was a pea-green 1954 Ford station wagon that my father bought used – not "pre-owned" as car sales folks like to say – but used ... VERY used. Her anti-aerodynamic appearance made it seem as if she was always standing still, even when she was going 50 miles per hour – probably her top speed.

Betsy took us on many road trips. Each summer, we would pack all our camping gear into a big wooden box my father had fastened to her roof, and all six of us kids would pile inside to make our annual vacation trip to Promised Land State Park in the Pocono Mountains. Each time we went, we spent the night before, sleeping on a mattress in Betsy's cargo space. We would wake up with my father already on the road, wheels humming below us. It was an exciting time for a young boy who learned to appreciate road trips before they were called road trips.

On one voyage, my father was forced to stop abruptly when a deer ran in front of us. The inertia let loose the moorings of the big wooden box and it – along with all the stuff inside of it – shot out in front of us, not even hitting the car's hood! We spent the next hour cleaning up all the stuff scattered on the road, much of which was broken.

It was not a great moment, but it is a great memory.

SUNDAY DRIVES

Every week during the spring and fall, my father would take us kids on "Sunday drives." These were aimless forays into the unknown, exploring back roads around Wilkes-Barre, Scranton, and beyond. We would be gone for hours. I think Daddy did this to allow my mother some "me time," without the cacophony of "Mommy"-this and "Mommy"-that to wear her down.

Although these trips were unstructured, there were two rules:

First, each kid took a turn deciding which road to turn onto as we traveled. The rule was that Daddy was required to take that route – no questions, no complaints, no alternatives. It got us into some very interesting and often ridiculous situations.

Second, at noon we had to stop and eat at the very next restaurant we passed – no questions, no complaints, no alternatives. We ate in many diners, some clean, and many hot dog stands and ice cream shops. We also dined at a few places where my father riffled through his wallet before we went in to make sure he had enough money to pay the bill.

Along the way, we took in the scenery, people-watched, and barely missed a lot of deer. To keep our minds active, Daddy urged us to play games. They didn't have names, just descriptions.

"Let's look for letters," my sister Barbara would announce. So we scoured the passing landscape for billboards, business signs, and other more creative sources, searching for the letter "A" at the beginning. Then "B" and "C". The letters "S" and "Y" were easy, for we came upon many "STOP" and "YIELD" road signs. However, when we got to "N" we knew we were close to (shudder) "Q". Often that would end our search, although every once in a while we ran across the word "Quality" on a sign. And once we passed a housing development called "Quail Acres."

Another game was a favorite of my brother David.

"License plates!" he would yell, and we competed with each other to keep score of the number of out-of-state plates attached to passing cars. This worked best on the busier highways.

"Colors!" our youngest brother Eddie would yell. So we looked for the number of cars within each color category we could find. This resulted in a few arguments about whether burgundy was red or blue, whether white cars were really a color, or whether black cars had bank robbers in them. We were very creative like that.

To this day, I sometimes turn down a street that I've never been on before, or I find myself looking for letters, noticing out-of-state license plates, and even counting colors. It makes me feel warm all over again, although I sometimes eye black cars with suspicion.

ROAD TRIPS WITH RAY:

His name was Ray – just Ray. I never learned his last name, but he's the one who turned me on to road trips. Ray was an acquaintance of a family that included my friend, Jackie Sweeney. For years, we camped near each other at Promised Land State Park. When I was 15, Jackie excitedly told me that Ray was taking him on a trip to Canada.

"Do you want to come along?" he asked.

Of course I did, although I was a little afraid to go that far into the unknown.

"Sure!" I said.

Ray owned an old DeSoto sedan. It was roomy and comfortable and looked like a big bubble floating down the highway. We were planning on a two-week journey, camping all along the way. With us, were two friends of Ray's – a woman, whose name I have forgotten – and her daughter, Julie, who was my age. I instantly fell in love with her.

Packed into that car, along with the baggage, were me, Julie, and Jackie in the back seat; Julie's mother in the passenger seat; and Ray driving. We headed north, visiting Niagara Falls, Quebec, and many points of interest in between.

When we returned, I was sold on road trips – and on Julie.

A FINE PAIR:

For a very long time while living in the village of Centermoreland, Pennsylvania, we owned two cars, both station wagons. The smaller one was a 1963 two-tone red and white Chevy II, mostly driven by my mother. The larger Chevrolet Bel Air, also a 1963 model, was my father's. It was all white.

Those cars saw our then-family of 10 through many adventures, right through my teenage years. When I began to drive, I usually took the Bel Air.

I eventually inherited the Chevy II. At the time I was in a bluegrass band – "Chaz Bones and the Endless Mountain Boys." We had been practicing at a friend's house north of Tunkhannock and were headed back home. The roads were slick with ice and I told everyone to make sure they buckled their seatbelts. I heard several snap together.

Coming down a long hill among farms just before entering town, the car lost its grip on the road. Out of control, we spun around and found ourselves traveling backwards at 40 miles an hour. As the road gently curved to the left, the car continued to go straight, bouncing over the berm at the shoulder and plowing through a field of just-cut corn stalk stubble.

When the car stopped, for a brief moment there was complete silence, then I heard one of my bandmates frantically scrambling to buckle his seatbelt, even though the horsepower had already left the barn.

That car didn't last long. I sold it to a junkyard dealer who told me to drive it in among the thousands of rusting vehicle carcasses and park it. I noticed that in some places, cars were piled in stacks, sometimes 10 high. It reminded me of that farmland art project in Amarillo, Texas where a landowner "planted" a line of vintage Cadillacs nose down in the ground. It's called Cadillac Ranch and has become quite the tourist attraction for road warriors. I decided to create my own art project and give the car – and me – one last thrill. I sped up just a bit and crashed into one of the stacks, and the cars tumbled over in a mighty crunch of metal. Luckily they fell away from me, not on me. I walked back to the entrance and bid a "thank you" to the owner. He hadn't even noticed the wreckage.

WILD HORSES:

My sister Barbara needed a car. I needed a car. But our family was living in Lake Winola, near Scranton, while I was in my first year at Bloomsburg State College (now a university), about 60 miles away.

Our father bought us a car – one car. Amazingly, it was a metallic blue 1965 Ford Mustang convertible, but it came with rules: While I was at college during the week, Barb would have the car. On weekends, when I came home, it was mine. It was the only truly cool car I ever had. I was surprised about how easy it was to pick up girls in that car. I don't know if Barb had the same experience with boys. I'd like to think she did.

BUGGED:

It was the first car I bought myself, with my own money. The $1,200 I had saved up got me the car of my "hippie" dreams – a 1968 yellow Volkswagen Beetle convertible with mag wheels, only two years old. I thought it was the most beautiful thing in my world.

One day, while driving around Wilkes-Barre, near where I lived, with the top down and my long hair flowing in the wind, I spotted a billboard advertising a local car dealership – a Volkswagen dealership. It featured a side view of a young man with long flowing hair, wearing a flowered shirt and a big smile, and driving a yellow Beetle convertible.

An idea burst from my brain.

The next day, I drove to that dealership, asked to see the manager, and offered to simply drive around with a magnetic sign on the side of my car advertising his business – for $50 a week. I even rummaged around in my closet where I found a purple and white flowered shirt, similar to the one on the billboard, to wear while driving, and I wore it to our meeting. The owner declined my generous offer but commended me on my ingenuity.

"Your car's just a little too old," he said. "I'd need you to drive a brand new one ... I could sell one to you."

I declined.

The funny thing about those Beetles, more often called bugs, is that they had no radiator. The engine was air-cooled. However, I learned the hard way that even an air-cooled engine needs oil. While driving on back roads off the Pennsylvania Turnpike interchange at Hickory Run State Park, I noticed that my red oil light was on. I chose to ignore it. Several miles later, the engine began to sputter. I passed a service station near the Turnpike interchange, but ignored it, then headed up a steep hill through a wooded area, where the engine coughed its last breath, and died.

I tried to turn the car around so I could coast back down to the service station, but I ended up with the car blocking the lane of travel. I couldn't push it around because of the hill's steepness and the car's angle. I couldn't move. I gathered all my valuables and belongings, suitcase, and such, then carried it into the woods where I hid all that stuff under some branches and behind a big rock. I figured that the car was a goner and I didn't want to lose all my stuff. There was nothing left for me to do but sit down on the bug's running board and dig into a pie that my mother had given to me earlier that day.

One car passed me, slowed down, but didn't stop. A few minutes later, a State Trooper showed up. He turned on his warning lights, got out of his car, strode briskly over to where I was eating, and said, "What the hell are you doing?!"

"Having some pie. Want some?"

That's probably what got me the ticket.

The cop called for a tow truck, which arrived minutes later, sent by the manager of the service station I had ignored earlier. When he tried to charge me $200 for the towing fee, and much more to fix the car, I said, "How about if I just give you the car?"

"That would be fine," he said.

I called my father, who picked me up after driving several hours to my location. He was irritated but grew amused on the way home while listening to my woeful tale.

The next day, I returned to the service station and turned over the papers and ownership of my favorite car. Then I drove up the hill – in my father's car – to retrieve all my stuff.

To this day I still wonder what happened to that car.

LOSS OF A LOVED SON AND NEPHEW:

I was stationed in Panama in 1992 when I got the awful news that my sister's youngest son, Jason Gumble, had died in a car crash. He had just earned his driver's license but was unskilled at negotiating curves during the fall when the roads around Lake Wallenpaupack where he lived were covered in wet leaves. The car slid into a tree.

I felt helpless because I couldn't go to the funeral to support my sister Barbara. We were – and still are – each other's confidants.

I was assigned as the non-commissioned officer of the U.S. Army South Public Affairs Office. As such, one of my duties was to write occasional pieces for the "Tropic Times" newspaper, which served the military and now-defunct Panama Canal Zone communities.

I decided to put Jason's loss into words, so I wrote a column about him and the crash. I even included a photo of the wreckage, although I don't remember how I got it. Seeing that story in print helped salve my wounds and drew me even closer to Barbara, at least in spirit. It was a defining family moment.

I've learned over the years that cars can be both a blessing and a curse. Without them, we are lost or, more to the point, stranded. With them is the financial baggage they carry – gas, maintenance, tolls, tires, and replacement parts. Also, there is the danger, with tragedy waiting around every corner if you're not paying attention. In the end, though, no matter the route chosen, all road trip adventures inevitably reach the letter "Z".

*   *   *

(Whew Tony! That is quite a long ride down memory lane. It is a memoir told through cars and the impact they have had on your life. I get very attached to the few cars we have owned. We traveled and camped a lot over the years, so our cars were like a part of our family. Most trips were usually fun and uneventful ...however ... we did have one that was a little unusual ... read on. – Becky)

CHAPTER 20

A Yugoslavian Adventure: The Stuff of Nightmares!

Becky

"You have to be going to a pretty awful place,
if getting there is half the fun."

– Miss Piggy
(From "The Muppet Show")

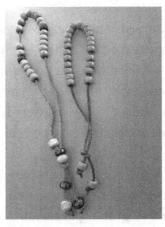

Worry beads.

*S*ometimes the stuff we cherish most dearly isn't stuff at all. Instead, it is the memory of experience; of adventure, travel, and even terror. It sticks with us – solid and real – like a little souvenir we might stuff in our pocket and carry back home.

In June of 1975 Ralph, our seven-year-old Scott, and I were heading off for a nice long camping vacation to Greece. At the time, we were living in Stuttgart, Germany on the Essingers' farm in Aldingen. Ralph was stationed at Robinson Barracks. We were very excited; we love road trips!

We threw our tent, sleeping bags, stove, a hammer, and Scott in the back of the car and headed off to see the world. We wanted to see Athens and some Greek islands.

Salzburg, Austria was our first stop where we camped near the salt mines. Next, we drove through a small piece of Italy and hit Yugoslavia heading toward Zadar. The route we chose was very mountainous with winding roads that were beautiful to look at but tortuous to drive, but we really wanted to travel along the coast and enjoy the scenery.

On a tiny two-lane road, we saw a smashed guard rail, a car lodged in a tree, and a lifeless body flanked by emergency workers. We gasped as the sight of that tragic scene came barreling unexpectedly into our "happy road trip" thoughts. I stopped singing. We drove in silence, and Ralph very carefully steered through the next hairpin turn.

That night we camped, then headed toward Split the next morning. The landscape turned rocky and orange as rust-hued rocks replaced the pine trees of the day before. We stopped to walk around the marketplace surrounded by a wall dating from 300 CE. We could hardly believe that the houses we passed were five centuries old! We bought Scott a pipe flute at the market so he could entertain us during the long car ride.

Next came Dubrovnik's city center where we looked up to see a gigantic teapot-shaped trailer driving down the main street. We guessed it was maybe a float in a parade, or an advertisement. We stayed a good distance behind so we could see and take photos of this colorful vision moving down the road. Suddenly sparks flew in the air above the top of the teapot. It seemed to have hit a telephone pole, along with overhanging wires on the busy street. As it pulled to the side, we passed slowly and continued on our way. We could see out our back window that the "fireworks" display had finished sparking, and people were gathering around the scene.

We stopped for a snack at a little roadside place and were talking to some tourists about how slippery the roads in Yugoslavia are when they are wet. They explained that it was because the pavement is mixed with marble chips. Actually, we weren't quite sure what they said, but we did listen closely when they told us to be careful because the roads were very slick. They knew that we were continuing into mountainous terrain ahead.

As we maneuvered along our tiny ribbon of road, flanked by rock on one side and cliffs on the other, it began to rain. With every hairpin turn, we held our breath. At five miles per hour, I began wondering how long it would take us to drive the stretch of Yugoslavia I had marked on the map. I was frightened. Ralph was nervous. Scott stopped playing the flute.

We came out of one tight turn to see men in vests gathered on the other side of the road looking outward. A big chunk of guard rail was missing. We could only imagine what had just happened. Ralph slowed to a crawl, and a white fruit and vegetable truck passed us on the left. We thought the truck was going a little fast, but we figured the driver must be familiar with the roads. We chugged along when, minutes later, we found ourselves dodging cabbages, turnips, apples, and then came upon the overturned fruit truck. The driver simply motioned us to pass.

About half an hour later we came to a bridge, and when we looked down beyond the railing, we saw a car that had taken a nose-dive into the water. Again, a big piece of guard rail was missing and people were standing on the side looking down. We crawled along. As we continued, my fear was being replaced with tears dripping down my face. Then the heavens opened up and a hard rain poured down. I kept repeating a mantra of, "Slow Down. Slow Down. Slow down."

while Ralph kept repeating, "The car won't go any slower!" The only time he pressed on the accelerator was when the road took steep upward climbs.

We kept going, and I still didn't believe we had just seen four serious accidents right before our eyes. As Ralph steered our car to the left to follow the road around yet another curve … our car did not turn! It continued straight. Then, very abruptly, it slid sideways up an embankment. It seemed as if the acceleration increased as our car took an upward flight. Our eyes widened at the sight before us – nothing but sky! We were in the air with our headlights pointing straight to heaven.

I tried to scream but nothing came out of my mouth. I held my breath. I looked to see Scott seated in the back seat. And E-V-E-R-Y-T-H-I-N-G … STOPPED. Not a sound; not a movement; just a complete pause, along with only one thought.

"This is it. It's over now."

But just as I resigned myself to the sad end of our Being, the front tires grabbed the big rocky embankment and Ralph regained control, steering the car back onto the ribbon road to safety.

We sat for a few minutes with flashers blinking, just to give us time to recover. It was hard to breathe. I had never felt so frightened and relieved in the same instant. Scott yelled a "WOW" from the back seat. Ralph just shook, then carefully put the car into gear and we proceeded at an even slower pace. I repeated my "Slow Down" mantra. I swore if we ever made it out of here alive I would never return, ever. This is not the stuff of which dreams are made.

Then, just like something out of a dream, I saw a sign advertising "The International Hotel." Frugal as we tend to be when traveling, I begged Ralph to pull into the parking lot.

"Look", I said," We need a nice shower, rest, and a meal. Tomorrow we can start all fresh and new."

It was still raining. To continue this drive in the dark of night would be insane.

We splurged and checked into the fancy hotel. The room was big. The beds looked soft. Covered with dust from the road and salted with sweat from the terrifying side trip off the road toward heaven, I went to check out the shower. I turned it on. A trickle of boiling water came out. No cold water. Then it produced a tiny mix of boiling and cold. I put shampoo on my hair. Then it was back to a trickle.

I yelled to Ralph to go to the front desk to tell them we have no water. He returned with a bucket filled with water. He said there was no water pressure, but they were working on it. We would have water in the morning. They told him to come back if he needed more water. I poured a few buckets into the bottom of the shower, and Scott took a bath. I used the trickle of shower water and another bucket of water to at least get some of the shampoo rinsed out of my hair. Ralph went into the bathroom and yelled for me to get another bucket of water. The toilet didn't flush. It was good exercise filling and carrying buckets. When we turned out the lights we thought about how nice it would be in the morning when the water was restored. It wasn't. Our trickle disappeared entirely.

In the lobby, there was one bathroom with water pressure that we could use to brush our teeth. Everyone in the hotel had to use this one room. Breakfast came with the room. We had some bread and juice and hard-boiled eggs. We asked at the desk if we could get a discount on the room. After all, we had no toilet, no shower, no water. Sadly, he said, "No."

Outside, when we again took to the snaking road, everything had brightened up. The sun was shining, and – despite our waterless ordeal – we were well rested.

We soon left the scary mountain roads and were happily visiting little villages and markets along the still-narrow trek. We finished off a whole roll of film, capturing the beauty of each of our stopping points. People, horse-drawn wagons, cows, goats. One farmer posed next to his oxen. He gave us his address hoping we would send him the photo. Yes, of course we would! We were feeling great. We bought some cheeses and bread and sausage, and stopped in a big field for a picnic. Ralph took the used roll of film and tucked it in his shirt pocket. We talked about how great it will be to remember the good parts of Yugoslavia in those snapshots.

Unfortunately, later that evening, Ralph discovered the roll of film was gone. It must have fallen out of his shirt. I kept thinking of that farmer waiting for the photo, and I felt terrible. That roll of film was in the category of "irretrievable stuff."

To change the mood, I happily announced we were only hours away from the Greek border. Sunshine and happiness were all around, and we didn't see one accident that day. It was just a short jaunt through the corner of Albania. However, after stopping in a small village south of Dubrovnik, we discovered that we could not drive through Albania. No one was allowed to drive through Albania. Oops! We now had to find a road – through more of Yugoslavia – that would take us to Greece.

Our maps showed no such road that could take us to the central highway and on toward Greece. We stopped at a store and asked how to get there. They gave us a map that showed a new road being built. We followed the map. That map led us right back into the mountains with even more dangerous drop-offs! Once again, we had reached the highest point of fright. Silently, but with mouths agape, we stared out at the winding road and mountains. We saw no gas stations, and no places to change money. We had no choice but to press on, and pray!

Finally, miraculously, we made it through and camped next to the border of Greece. Early the next morning, we crossed over and changed our money, but some of our Yugoslavian bills were too big for them to accept. We trudged back across the border to Yugoslavia to change our bills to smaller denominations. Scott was amazed that he got 390 drachmas for his nine American dollars.

We continued to follow mountainous roads through Greece and camped at Delphi, visited its museum, and saw the city's ancient ruins. Then we headed for Athens. The city was congested with traffic, so we camped the night and explored by bus the next day. We took a subway to the Acropolis, snapping photos of everything we saw. We held onto those rolls of film with all our might, for the stuff of memory was on every frame.

It was a busy day in Athens. We stood on the steps of the Parthenon, walked to and through Hadrian's Arch, then off to the zoo, and finally to the Parliament Building to see the changing of the guards in Grecian kilts. We managed to see the Archeological Museum the next day. At a tourist bureau, we found brochures describing the Greek Islands. We looked them over while snacking on meat pies, baklava, and tea at an outdoor café. Then we shopped. Our first purchase was a set of Worry Beads. We would need them if we ever found ourselves back in Yugoslavia. We shopped and bought little pieces of stuff we hoped to keep forever – all Good Stuff.

We went to the Peloponnese Peninsula first and then back to see more islands. We went to Mycenae and visited the amphitheater in Epidaurus. To test the amazing acoustics in that ancient venue, I dropped a tiny plastic lipstick cap while standing in the middle of the stage. Scott and Ralph could hear it fall from where they stood far away in the last row at the top of the theater. Then we saw Agamemnon's Tomb. We also spent a lot of time on the beach. Scott snorkeled around trying to catch fish with his bare hands. He was probably imagining that he was hunting sharks because of a book he had been reading – "Jaws." Our last sight to see was the Temple of Poseidon in Sounion.

The following day we were on the ferry to Mykonos from Piraeus. We strolled along the narrow walkways that led us to a hotel where the path dead-ended at a staircase. There stood our hotel. It was terrible! Our room had two very old rusty metal beds and a ceramic vase on the wall with rusty water dripping down the side. The bathroom was on the roof. It was just a hole in a wooden box, no seat, and a bucket next to it with a sign that said "Put paper in the waste basket."

We told the owner we could not stay. She said if we could stay just one night, she would get us a place with running water, and shower ... tomorrow. I was sure she told us this because it was the only way anyone would actually pay to stay in this dump. We stayed the night.

The next morning, I decided we needed to get off that island fast! I had seen enough of Mykonos and couldn't wait for the ferry to rescue us from this island. Meanwhile, we sought out some diversion to keep us occupied until boarding time that evening. We decided to take a 20-minute bus ride to a beach. We enjoyed the afternoon on the sand and in the water and then noticed a little outdoor restaurant just a short distance away. We ordered freshly caught fish, and the owner came over to the table to talk. I asked if there was a hotel or someplace close by where we could stay. He said he had rooms to rent. It was a little motel. We quickly reserved a room for the rest of our time on Mykonos. Our room looked out over the beach and the Mediterranean Sea.

We returned to that same place every year. We know there are other islands that are charming and that we should explore them; but once we found our paradise … what more is there to search for? By the way, when we took our yearly visits to Mykonos, we flew! The trip was much faster and filled with much less anxiety.

This first trip to Greece was overflowing with emotions ranging from awe to fright; calm to euphoria, and I remember the entire adventure every time I glance at the stuff I brought home – especially my Worry Beads.

* * *

(Becky, that was a frightful, vacation! But certainly memorable. I've never been to Yugoslavia, although I did skirt by it once. When I read your take on the conditions of the roads, it brought me back to a staircase of switchbacks in the Dolomite Mountains. Let's stick to the road through the following "moving" memory, stuffed with humor. It's not about a vacation full of trepidation, but about an awkward change of assignment without a change of clothes! – Tony)

CHAPTER 21

A Military 'Debriefing'

Tony

"Trying to be happy by accumulating possessions is like trying to satisfy hunger by taping sandwiches all over your body."

– George Carlin
(American stand-up comic)

A warning sign keeps movers honest.

*I*n the July-August 2023 edition of "Reader's Digest," in the regular "Humor in Uniform" feature, a military veteran talks about stuff that should have been dumped but wasn't. It's something all military families both enjoy and endure; the excitement that comes from the prospect of living in a new place, and the awfulness of the move itself.

After overly efficient movers swarmed into this vet's home, and after his stuff arrived at his new home, his family discovered – boxed neatly away – a brick that had held the door open as the movers carried everything to their truck. It was an unintended passenger, a stowaway. They also found a bag of rotting garbage stuffed among their valuable belongings.

When my family made our first move overseas to Bremerhaven, Germany, we had a similar, more troublesome, experience. We had yet to learn from more experienced military families that if there's anything you don't want the movers to take away, you had better put it in the bathtub and close the shower curtain. Military contract movers tend to descend on your home like locusts. The ritual of the bathtub prevents the swarm of movers from carrying off the stuff you'll need before you arrive at your next duty station.

Sometimes, during your debriefing when you arrive at your new duty station, you can complain about movers who pack your garbage and open pickle jars, but that doesn't stop the locusts from taking it in the first place.

We weren't expecting them to arrive so early that morning at our government quarters on Fort Devens, Massachusetts. I hadn't even dressed yet, and all my clothes were laid out on the bed. Wearing a bathrobe, I answered the door and four burly men swarmed in. Their leader had me sign some paperwork while the others had already begun to tear into our belongings.

They made quick work of it. Although we tried to stay out of their way, we were also constantly running in front of them, picking up this and that so they wouldn't stuff it into their truck.

When they finished, and left, I was still in my bathrobe. We were all pretty hungry by that time and planned to go to our favorite restaurant one last time before we shipped out. I went to the bedroom to get dressed. When I went over to the bed, now stripped of its sheets and blankets, I couldn't find my clothes. No blue jeans, no Hawaiian shirt, no shoes. Mary had to go to the PX to buy a new set of clothes so that I could leave the house.

Weeks later, in Bremerhaven, I would discover that the movers had wrapped my duds in the bed sheets and whisked them all away.

Sometimes your stuff is really important. In this case, even my underwear was missing. I had been debriefed by the military!

* * *

(Tony! Usually moving day is a day filled with stress and anxiety. You managed to make your moving day hilarious! When I read about your missing items, it made me think about the time our items were not. Read on. – Becky)

CHAPTER 22

Amsterdam, Versailles, and Rejected Stuff

Becky

"I still believe, in spite of everything, that people are truly good at heart."

– Ann Frank
    (A young Jewish girl in hiding during WWII)

Beautiful Versailles.

*D*uring our time living in Nuremberg, Germany from 1986 to 1991, Ralph and I, and our two younger kids – Jason, 11, and Natanya, 10 – traveled quite a bit. Scott, our oldest, was at Washington University in St. Louis traveling toward his degree in structural engineering. Our Toyota van, known by our neighbors as the Silver Bullet, transported us all over Europe, and we thoroughly enjoyed visiting the many places we had always dreamed of seeing. Occasionally we dealt with a few negatives. They always seemed to end in laughter, because we just cannot allow the unimportant stuff to matter.

Amsterdam is a beautiful city with flower markets, houseboats along the canals, a world-famous diamond district, and endless museums and landmarks. We parked our van on the street that morning and spent the entire day walking the city and seeing everything that we had highlighted on our map. Late that afternoon, we went to see Ann Frank's house and took the last tour. It was an interesting and touching experience. We saw the hidden entrance behind a bookcase that led to the small living space where Ann and her family, and another Jewish family, were hidden from 1942 to 1944 during the WWII German occupation of the Netherlands. Their hiding place was discovered by the Nazis, and Ann and her family were transported to Auschwitz. She and her sister were transferred to Bergen-Belsen where they both died just months before the war ended. After the war, the young girl's account of those years of hiding was found and published as "The Diary of Ann Frank." The book ends with her words, "I still believe, in spite of everything, that people are truly good at heart."

On the way back to the van it began to drizzle. As I walked briskly along the wet sidewalk, I noticed papers scattered along the road as we approached our van. On closer observation, I saw they were OUR papers! I was shocked to see our insurance card, our ADAC insurance packet, and maps...

"Ralph" I called back to him as he walked at a slower pace flanked by the kids. "Our papers are all over the ground!"

We got to the van and saw that someone had broken into the car and must have been looking for something. The glove compartment was open, along with the ashtray and our ice chest. Our stuff was all rearranged.

"Oh nooo, where is my Walkman?" Jason yelled as he jumped into the back seat and looked under jackets and books that had been thrown on the floor.

"It's here in the front seat," I said. He gathered it and all his tapes with a smile of relief.

Ralph thought maybe the radio cassette stereo system he had installed had been taken, but no, it was all there. Our stuff had been rearranged, but everything was fine.

We knew there had been a few attacks on Americans traveling in Europe. We were easy targets because the Army issued Americans overseas green license plates for our cars, not the European white ones. We were a little worried that maybe the intruders had tampered with our car. We looked around the car and under the hood, and although we did not know what we were looking at, it all seemed fine. Ralph turned the key, and after the uneventful sound of the engine catching, we continued on our way.

When we happened to see a policeman walking on the street, we mentioned the annoying invasion to him. He told us that car thieves are usually looking for loose diamonds that Americans purchase in the Diamond District and stick in their glove compartments or somewhere hidden in their cars while they tour the city. The only damage for us was the broken lock on the car door.

A few months later, we jumped into the van to explore France. Versailles was our destination. We parked in a huge, guarded gravel lot right in front of the gates of the beautiful Palace. The tour was nice, the gardens were breathtakingly beautiful. It was a hot sunny day, and when we headed to the van to leave we could not wait to get a cool drink from our ice chest.

Ralph put the key in the good lock, but it was broken. We opened the other side and peeked in. We noticed right away that once again everything had been rearranged, and once again Ralph's speakers and sound system were still there. Nothing was missing, but we had another broken lock on our van. If we had one more break-in we would have to climb into the hatch in the back of the van to enter.

As we settled into our seats, I noticed a man lifting a tiny child into the window of a car a few aisles over from where we were. The child was rummaging around the inside of the car while the man stood looking around to make sure no one was coming.

I got out of the van, walked over to the guard station, and yelled through his little window, "There is a man and his little boy breaking into cars here. We just saw him lift his boy through a window. Our car too was vandalized by this guy and his kid."

The guard looked at me and shrugged his shoulders. "Yes, it happens every five minutes. What can I do?"

I wanted to shout at him at the top of my lungs, "Maybe you should blow your whistle or tell them to leave, or escort them off the premises!" ... but I held my tongue. His lack of concern made me think I should just hurry and leave.

As we were pulling out of the UN-GUARDED parking lot, our pre-teen daughter leaned over the seat and said, "I feel sorry for Dad. People keep breaking into our van and no one wants any of his stuff."

I chuckled, but then never thought about it much until we were writing this book about stuff. Now it seems so appropriate to include this. We thought we had collected some very cool stuff, only to have it all rejected by the thieves of Europe!

*　*　*

(Becky, that story makes me feel angry! How can people do that sort of thing, and with a little child as an accomplice? And how can supposedly protective officials do nothing about it? When I think of that moment, it stirs up yet another bad memory about the time I was robbed in Vienna, Austria ... at knifepoint ... while I was pushing my mother in a wheelchair! I felt like throwing rocks at them! But I knew better. Besides, part of me has a special affinity for rocks. Follow this next story, and trust me, it's only a stone's throw from the truth. – Tony)

CHAPTER 23

Rocks of Ages

Tony

"There will always be rocks in the road ahead of us.
They will be stumbling blocks or stepping stones;
it all depends on how you use them."

– *Friedrich Nietzsche*
(19th-century German philosopher)

Tony's piece of the Berlin Wall.

*W*hen I was about 12, I thought I wanted to be a geologist when I grew up. It began with me bending over in our family's half-mile long driveway off Lower Demunds Road in Dallas, Pennsylvania.

It was just a small thing – a white oval stone, smooth to the touch, and freckled, like me. I blew some of the road dust off it and dropped it into my pocket. From there, it went into my sock drawer in my room in our "House on the Hill," as we called our home on 73 acres of mostly forested land. But we also had cliffs that hunkered over a copse of trees, and at the bottom of those rough faces were caves, and within those caves were piles of rocks.

It came as a flash the instant my sock drawer, now holding my little treasure, slid shut.

"I'm going to collect rocks," I decided, which is how I ended up scurrying around in the caves with a flashlight and a rapidly growing bag full of stones. Some were rust colored, some black, and green, purple, and white. Some sparkled (I later learned that cube-shaped find was pyrite, fool's gold.). Others were rough; their shapes and sizes as varied as their colors. One in particular drew more of my interest than the others. It was green and triangular, with rounded points, and the surface felt crumbly. I put that one in my pocket.

On my hike back to the house after my first day exploring the caves – not as a spelunker, but as a budding geologist – I thought about what I could do with my collection. The drawer where I put my first find would only hold so many. Besides, my mother probably wouldn't appreciate me turning my sock drawer into a rock drawer. Also, I wanted to show them off, not hide them in the dark. Then I thought about the museum my sixth-grade class visited on a field trip before summer vacation. "I need a display case," I thought, and my mind went into action, searching for a solution.

When I got home, I told my father about my new hobby. He seemed amused but was encouraging.

"I have just the thing," he said when I told him I was looking for some way to show off my collection. He took me into his garage workshop and dug out a gold-painted metal screen about five feet tall and three feet wide, with short legs to hold it upright. The flat surface was filled with holes.

"You can use wire or string to attach your rocks to one side," he suggested. "Then you can set it up in the corner of your room."

"That's a great idea, Daddy," I said, and I immediately set to work.

It didn't take long to fasten the rocks to the screen, although it took days for me to decide which ones to mount on this place of honor. But when finished, my display was as impressive as I imagined it should be. There were about 40 rocks on the screen. The round ones were especially difficult because they had no sharp edges for the tiny cages fashioned from the wire my father gave me to gain purchase. I put the leftover rocks into a sock, whose partner had long ago disappeared into laundry limbo, and threw it into the sock drawer.

My father had a friend who was a geologist. One day, while he was visiting us, my father mentioned my collection.

"Can I see it?" he asked, and I proudly led him up to my room, with my father tagging along behind. With a grand "ta-da!" hand gesture, I directed the geologist to my screen. He began identifying each one by type – sedimentary, igneous, volcanic, and something called conglomerate. I showed him the one that started me down this road – the white one with the freckles.

"That's quartz," he said, adding, "You know, I have a book in my car that I'll give to you. It's all about identifying different kinds of rocks, and ...."

Suddenly, he stopped and bent down to peer at my green, crumbly rock that I had so carefully carried home in my pocket. I didn't want the wire to damage it so I placed it in a small, clear jewelry bag my mother had given to me and ran the wire through that.

"Hello. What's this?" he asked, more to himself than to me. "May I touch it?"

I removed it from the screen, opened the bag, and handed it to him. From his pocket, he pulled out a small magnifying glass to study it more closely. "Where did you get this?" he asked. He seemed more serious all of a sudden, but excited.

"In a cave on our property," I said.

Turning to my father, he asked, "Would you mind if I come back on the weekend and bring some of my tools? I'd like to see this cave."

"Sure," my father said, adding, "But what's so special about that rock?"

"Well, I'm not sure yet, but I don't think this is a rock. I believe it might be a fossil – a dinosaur fossil."

"Really?!" I gushed.

"Now don't get excited yet," he laughed, "We don't know for sure. It needs more study."

It was too late, though, and I completely ignored his cautious point that it might just be a crumbly rock with a green complexion, but I was excited beyond a rock collector's dream.

"Was it a Tyrannosaurus Rex?" I asked breathlessly. We had been studying dinosaurs in school and I hoped for an immediate T-Rex affirmation from my father's friend.

He looked closer at the object in his hand, now seemingly more valuable than gold, then said, "Slow down, Tony. We don't even know if it is a dinosaur bone. It might not be that old ... It could even be human."

My father seemed disturbed by this revelation but didn't say anything.

"... but if you want," his friend continued, "I suppose you can pretend it's a T-Rex – at least until we learn the truth. May I take this with me to study it?"

I really didn't want to let it go, but my father convinced me that it would be well cared for.

"Okay," I said. "I guess so."

That was the last I saw of my little green rock. I imagine it is archived in a small box in a drawer of a museum laboratory somewhere, or perhaps it's joined once again to the Earth, having been thrown out because it wasn't a T-Rex after all; it was just a green rock, perhaps not a fossil at all. Maybe it was even in the geologist's sock drawer.

And the rest of my collection? Piece by piece, it came off the screen, a collection scattered to the ground, and even the screen itself is probably languishing in some landfill somewhere. Or maybe it's being put to some other use. And the rocks in my socks? Gone, I know not when nor where on Earth. Disappeared – just stuff turned to dust, like my dream of becoming a geologist.

Some 60 years later, I have a confession to make: I still have rocks scattered here and there throughout my home. They're not from that screen so long ago. They're kind of grownup rocks if you will. They arrive in my luggage after I return from traveling someplace new. I usually just pick up a stone from the ground. I look for the most unique one I can find within the small area around me at the time it strikes my fancy to grab one. As souvenirs, they are of my own making; my own decision. They're also cheap.

Included in what might loosely be described as my collection are also rocks given to me by others from their travels. They come from places I've never seen but I should have, could have, or wasn't able to but wanted to experience.

When my son Ian traveled to the Grand Canyon, I said, "Bring me back a bag of rocks." He did. There's about a half dozen of them in a little leather pouch hanging from a framed postcard he had sent from Arizona.

When my granddaughters, Greta and Renate, went to Yellowstone National Park, I said, "Bring me back a bag of rocks." They did. They're sitting on my desk in a brown paper bag waiting for me to decide where to put them..

When my wife Mary and I visited my best friend, Bradley Fuller, in Asheville, North Carolina, I picked up a couple of rocks from around his neighborhood. They're also sitting on my desk, right next to Greta and Renate's paper bag!

But my most prized rock is a chunk of concrete, larger than all my other rocks. It fits snugly into the palm of my hand and is painted on one side – graffiti art that once graced the Western side of the Berlin Wall. During a 1990 visit to Germany, I picked it up from the wall's rubble shortly after that most visible Cold War symbol fell, releasing a flood of humanity – and joy. It has a secure place of honor in my home, but for the life of me, I can't remember where I put it. Maybe I should look in my sock drawer.

*   *   *

(Oh Tony, I know that horrible frustration that follows your unfulfilled dream of becoming a geologist. Sometimes we are so sure we hear our calling, only to find out it is someone else's number that's being called. I thought I might stimulate future geologists during a visit with our grandkids in New Mexico many years ago. I am always amazed at how much I learn when hanging out with grandkids and their genuine, unfiltered, "un'adult'erated" logic. Read on. – Becky)

CHAPTER 24

Collecting Rocks for All to Enjoy

Becky

*To plant a garden
is to believe in tomorrow."*

*– Audrey Hepburn
(A Golden-Age-of-Hollywood actress)*

Rock collecting.

*I*n the summer of 2015 Ralph and I were off to Los Alamos, New Mexico to visit our daughter and family, including 6-year-old Ana and 3-year-old Oli. It is always such a joy to be with family and catch up on everything they have been doing during the time between visits. Weeks before the trip from Easton, Pennsylvania, my husband Ralph and I were busy gathering small presents to bring to the grandkids. During this process, we tried to think back to our own childhood years to see if there might be something special that stood out in our minds.

I remembered a rock collection that was given to me when I was a child. It came in a red square box. When I opened the box and looked inside, there was a white sheet of cardboard. Glued to the board were tiny rocks with the name of each specimen written in ink directly below it. My mother read their names aloud, and we looked them up in our new set of American People's Encyclopedia. Before that, I never even thought about rocks. They were just rocks. It was interesting to learn how they got here and what sort of ingredients were needed to make each one unique.

Ralph said he had the exact same rock collection when he was a kid and thought everyone in his neighborhood had one too. We thought the grandkids might enjoy them. We ordered two sets and popped them in our suitcases.

It was a fun-filled visit, and the little rock collections were a successful surprise. I also brought with me a tiny book entitled, "All About Rocks," that we read.

It was a beautiful sunny day, and the kids love to take walks, so we brought a bag to collect rocks along the way. The kids led us through the neighborhood and over to their Montessori school and to the playground. Every few steps they would both squat down to inspect some stones they had spotted and toss them in the bag.

Ana had learned to make Pine Needle Tea at the Montessori school, so we picked some pine needles too, and decided to go back to the house, have some tea, and look over our collection. The tea was good. Each of us held up a stone and said what we thought it was. We started to label them, but soon we had to put everything away because we had to get ready for dinner. Ana picked up all of the rocks we had inspected, put them in the bag, and walked out the front door with them.

"Where are you going, Ana?" I yelled after her.

She said she was going to put the rocks away. We followed her outside. She walked directly over to the tree in their front yard and dumped all the stones into the planter around it.

"Why did you do that?" I asked.

With a confused look, she explained, "Because that is where they belong. Where else would I put them?"

I said, "Maybe in your room?" which made her look even more confused.

She laughed and said, "Meema (Grandma), rocks belong outside. We can look at them any time, and now we know their names!"

It still makes me laugh when I think of how matter-of-fact and true that statement was. It left me wondering, "Why DO we keep rocks in a drawer when we can look at them anytime we want if they are right outside where they belong?"

*   *   *

(Becky, that is such a charming, rock-solid story. I'm not sure if you kept any rocks in your drawers, but if you had, you should have also used your sock drawer like me, because sometimes when you're hunting for rocks, you need an extra pair of socks, especially during a snowstorm in summer. I'd better explain. – Tony)

CHAPTER 25

An Unexpected Snowstorm

Tony

"Surprise is the greatest gift which life can grant us."

– *Boris Pasternak*
(Russian author, "Dr. Zhivago")

The 2002 Salt Lake City Olympic Games snow globe.

*I*n 2023, my daughter Bethany, her husband Joel, and our granddaughters, Greta, 15, and Renate, 13, took a summer trip out west. The family engages in German folk dancing called *Schuhplattler* (German for "Courtship Dance") and were off to Ohio for a gathering of similar-minded aficionados where different age groups from around the country danced for fun and competed for honors.

They traveled with all the stuff required to compete, right down to the girls' voluminous *Dirndls* (traditional German dresses) and Joel's feathered cap and *Lederhosen* (short leather pants). Renate, the youngest, is the most avid and accomplished dancer of the family. After she took fifth place in her competition, they extended their vacation to visit Yellowstone National Park.

The family usually travels to Germany for summer vacations. They can do so because Joel is a schoolteacher and has his summers off. But because of the Covid-19 pandemic restrictions still in place, they were unable to do so this year.

Before he married Bethany, Joel worked for the government's Bureau of Land Management in Montana and Wyoming. And because – at least in Joel's eyes – those far points were only a bison's stroll from Ohio, he decided to take a "side trip" to visit his old haunts.

Road Trip!

The family traveled with an additional pile of gear – the stuff of family camping. They were joined by a friend from the time when he and Joel worked together out west. I never met Mike Ford, but by all accounts he seemed to be a well-loved man, especially by Greta and Renate. Living closer to the national park in Salt Lake City, Mike set aside his schedule for a quick trip to join his longtime friend and family.

I knew Mike must have been very special. When the girls came to visit us after their trip, they told me, with great excitement, about Mike. Renate was especially impressed with him, and I knew he must be very special when that young lady described him, ending with, "*Opa* (grandpa), Mike is so cool! He's almost as cool as you are!"

She then paused, reconsidered how she had put that, and sheepishly added, "Almost."

The girls must have talked to Mike about my wife Mary and me, and they must have told him about how much their *Oma* (grandma) loves the Olympics. During the Olympic season, Mary is affixed to our TV, like a stamp on the envelope of a letter destined for a faraway and beautiful place.

A few weeks after they returned from the Rocky Mountains, a package arrived on our doorstep. It was from Mike Ford. Inside was an exceptionally well-made snow globe – the kind you shake to create blizzard conditions inside the glass. Within the globe was a replica of that year's Olympic flame atop the event's iconic five-ring logo. Around the globe's base was a tiny three-dimensional scene of a city skyline with snow-capped mountains in the distance. A little plaque on the base read, "Salt Lake City 2002." It had belonged to Mike's 94-year-old mother (I have since discovered that that globe is worth $40).

Mike sent this memento to Mary, without ever meeting, or knowing her. It was a gift out of the blue, a good chunk of the kind of stuff that plucks at the heartstrings. It was a remarkably sweet treat from the unknown.

As Mary turned this new prize over in her hands, shaking it and feeling its considerable heft, I looked on, wondering if indeed Mike Ford was cooler than I was.

POSTSCRIPT: On the day that I wrote this chapter, I was out in our garden, spreading mulch and picking squash and tomatoes. A woman pulled up in front of our house, got out of her SUV, and approached me.

"Are you the owner of this house?" she asked.

I thought, "Uh-oh, what kind of complaint is she going to lodge against me?" But that's not what she had in mind at all.

She said her name was Melinda and explained, "I just wanted to tell you that several years ago I picked up a snake-tongue plant you had put out next to your sign. It said, 'Free to a good home.' I took that plant to my mother's house in Lower Saucon Township (not far from our Hellertown location) and planted it there. Now we have three of them, and they're all this high," and she used the flat of her hand to indicate a spot at her chin level. "I saw you out here and I just had to stop and tell you how pleased I am that you did that, and to let you know how they're doing."

"Oh, well thank you," I said, and although I might not have shown it, she made me feel really good.

We chatted for a few moments, said goodbye, and she drove off, leaving me leaning on my garden rake and pondering this evidence that there are good people out there in the world. She made my day, perhaps my whole week, and she didn't give me a single thing; not a shred of stuff. But, like Mike Ford, she gave me an unexpected and wondrous surprise.

*   *   *

(Tony! She may not have given you anything tangible, but she did give you one thing for sure. She personally delivered a thank you for your thoughtfulness and your kindness. It is heartwarming to see a plant on someone's lawn with an offer to take it home. One day when I was taking a walk, I complimented a woman who was working in her garden at the front of her house. She said she would give me the seeds so I could plant them. The next time I walked by there was a bag of seeds for me perched on her fence. Sharing does make the world a more beautiful place.

I don't know if Mike is cooler than you, Tony, but he does have incredible skill in finding a perfect gift! – Becky)

134

CHAPTER 26

Valuable Trinkets, and Learning About Kid Stuff

Becky

"When you love what you have,
you have everything you need."

– Alan Alexander Milne, 1882-1956,
(English author of "Winnie-the-Pooh")

"Valuable" trinkets.

*I*t was 1980 and we had just moved to Blue Springs, Missouri, a suburb of Kansas City, and bought our first house. My husband Ralph was in a residency program for Pediatric Dentistry at the University of Missouri.

Our oldest son, Scott, was in junior high school. The two youngest might have been ready for preschool. It was a day filled with emotion as I headed over to Papa Claudet and Mrs. Ustard's Montessori School at the Little Red School House open house. According to age, Jason could begin school the following week. We were told that Natanya was a little too young for school because of her birth date. However, it was up to us to decide if we wanted to wait or enroll her early.

Jason's first day was not exactly what we expected. He was miserable and decided he would rather play on the swings than go to class. That meant poor Papa Claudet was stuck on a swing trying to convince him to enter the building. Four hours later when I returned, they were still swinging. Jason sprinted to the car like a released cheetah. It was a memorable day but for all the wrong reasons. Jason swore never to return to school – not ever. Natanya, who had returned home with me, cried all day because she wanted to go to school with Jason.

The next morning, I wisely dropped brother and sister off together. They were such happy little students as they both marched off to academia! I came back home to our empty house, sank into a cushioned chair, and listened intently to the quiet that I had not heard in years. Then I felt a complete rush of adrenaline as I sprang to my feet, put on my tennis shoes, and went for a mile run.

Returning home and vowing to use my time and energy wisely, I decided to clean out two baskets of trinkets and small toys at the bottom of the closet shared by the two preschoolers. With no distractions, I inspected each item for value and worth. The ones that failed my scrutiny were unceremoniously tossed. I was a child once so there was much consideration as to what might have emotional value. Tiny plastic things, mostly from fast food meals from long ago, with missing or broken parts, were easily discarded. The rest were tucked neatly back into the closet.

I picked the kids up that afternoon and listened as they bubbled over with excitement, telling me all that they had done that day. We came home, had a snack, and took a walk, stopping to meet new neighbors along the way. We had a jubilant re-run of the preschool events when Scott and Ralph returned a few hours later.

I began to cook dinner, Scott was doing homework, and Ralph sat reading the newspaper with eyes half closed. The younger ones were playing quietly in their room. Suddenly, and without warning, screams of horror exploded down the hallway. Red-faced and crying, my previously smiling preschoolers were now enraged.

"Our toys!! They're gone!! They both yelled as they ran down the hall, with exclamation marks flying through the air.

"Where's my favorite pumpkin key chain I got trick-or-treating?" Natanya sobbed.

"And where's my Happy-Meal clown with no arms?" screamed the other.

I leaned over to comfort them.

"Is that all that is missing?" I asked very quietly. "I'm sure we can get you another," I said confidently.

"NOOOO!" both wailed in unison and stomped their feet. "We want OUR toys!"

"Hmm ... Let me see if they're in the vacuum cleaner," I said as I scurried as fast as I could to the garage and dove into the huge plastic trash bin. Searching frantically, I heard other, deeper-voiced screams of distress from the kitchen above me.

"Are we eating any time soon?" grouched Ralph and Scott, and I thought I even heard their stomachs growling.

When I had finally retrieved the missing toys, I quietly tip-toed back to their closet, tossed the lost treasures into the baskets, and closed the door behind me. Maybe some things are off limits to my good intentions.

So, on this very special First Day of school, it seems my children taught me an important lesson about the value of trinkets and little broken pieces of Stuff!

*   *   *

(Becky. Your story about the value of broken things shows how smart kids can be. It's an amusing tale of wisdom. But those "broken pieces" of toys remind me of a heart-rending lesson I learned during my wife Mary and my early years of marriage. On the day of this story, I acted in anger, and held onto the stuff of anger too tightly, unable to set it free – like a little wounded bird that could no longer take flight. – Tony)

CHAPTER 27

A Bird in the Hand

Tony

*"You, like me, set more value on our personal
relationship than on our possessions."*

– Leo Emil Nauroth
      (Tony's father in a 1946 letter to his wife)

A fragile wooden bird.

Shortly after Mary and I married, and following a brief residency with my parents, we moved into a small bungalow near Harvey's Lake, Pennsylvania. We rented it from a retired Luzerne County judge, who also viewed himself as a gentleman farmer. Our home was small, but it had 16 windows, so the interior got a lot of light. Sometimes, however, it suffered from a lack of illumination.

The structure used to be the farmhands' bunkhouse, but that was back when the 100-acre property was a real farm, maybe even a ranch. The place had four small rooms and was heated by a cantankerous coal furnace that I regularly wrestled with.

It was 1972, and Mary and I had been married for only one year. Since we both attended Wilkes College in nearby Wilkes-Barre, we were financially thankful that we found this place. Although it was free, we did have to pay "rent" with the sweat off our backs. We constantly tended to the chores, mostly taking care of the judge's "livestock" – one horse, one cow, four chickens, and a rumble of cats. We also brought in hay from the fields, ran errands, and drove the farm pickup truck to fetch coal for both the bungalow and the main house.

In this lonely setting, Mary and I were still trying to find our footing in our relationship. Sometimes the tiny spaces we shared seemed more like a pressure cooker than a home. Sometimes we argued; sometimes we fought; often we made love.

When we were at school, during lunch, or between classes, we would meet with another couple who became good friends. Brent Spencer was, like me, an English major. Katie Houck was an artist, and Mary grew close to her. Brent and Katie were married, but Katie kept her maiden name at a time when such a bold move was only beginning to become acceptable.

One day, Katie gave Mary a present – probably for my wife's birthday. It was a small wooden bird Katie had carved and left unpainted. Raw wood. It had a tail that flared out behind it, and wings attached with very strong glue in slots she had cut just above each side of the little critter's breast. It was the perfect size, large enough to show detail; small enough to nest comfortably in the palm of Mary's hand. She loved that little bird.

Mary had grown up in a home where sometimes the cupboards held nothing but a jar of peanut butter, a bottle of ketchup, and a half-loaf of stale bread. Presents were few and far between, and even on Christmas Eve, Mary would wait with fading hope for a Christmas tree to appear in the apartment she shared with her mother and two of her five siblings.

Not long after Katie gifted Mary with the bird, we were alone in the bungalow. For some reason, an argument came slithering into our conversation, snaking around our hearts. I don't remember what we were fighting about because it's not memorable. It couldn't have been important. Our fights weren't physical. I would never hit her. Ever. But occasionally we argued with great vigor. When such "discussions" reached a crescendo, I would storm off by myself, sulking, angry, wanting to throw something through one of the 16 windows, but knowing I never would.

I stalked into the bedroom, sat down on the quilt, and stewed. I looked around the room, searching for something I could hit. Perhaps one of the pillows would do. Then, my eyes lit upon the little wooden bird sitting on Mary's nightstand. I reached over and plucked it up between my fingers. Turning it over in my hands, I admired Katie's craftsmanship – the smooth head and belly, the featherless back.

"Katie did a good job; a good thing for Mary," I thought.

Slowly, my usual calmness seeped back into my muscles, and I thought about going back into the living room to apologize. Then, a brief moment of rage returned. I held the bird, too tightly, as the rage built. I squeezed and wondered both when and if those tender wings would break.

"SNAP! SNAP!" Both gone, and they fluttered to the floor, more like stones than feathers. Despite my strange and horrid sense of satisfaction, remorse rushed in. So did Mary.

"What have you done!" she cried, grabbing the wingless body and inspecting the nubs where the wings had been attached. "Why did you do that, Tony?!" And she sobbed.

I began to apologize, now truly sorry for breaking one of the few things Mary ever owned; something she could – with definite assurance – call her own. If her heart weren't broken by my foolish act, it certainly was badly bruised.

"I'm sorry," I pleaded, and I reached out to hold her.

She would have none of it. Turning away, backing off, and still cupping the flightless body in her hand, she screamed, "I can never have anything, can I!" Then she rushed out of the room, out of the bungalow, and perhaps, I imagined, out of my life.

It's been years since that unfortunate episode, yet every once in a while I remember that terrible day. With great regret, I wonder how I had been such a cad. My heart aches during those times. Mary and I are still together – married for more than 50 years. Our fights are more intelligent; more meaningful. We talk, not yell. They say "love conquers all." That may be true. But it hasn't eased the pain of that memory.

Brent and Katie split up. Divorced. He is now a professor of English literature, teaching at a small college in the Midwest. He has published three books – "Are We Not Men?", "The Lost Son," and "Rattlesnake Daddy." Katie is gone from Brent's life; gone from ours. Who knows where she is or what she is doing. Perhaps I'll try to find her. Perhaps I can prod her into crafting a new little wooden bird for Mary's next Christmas. Or perhaps that little bird has become nothing more than stuff gone South.

* * *

(Tony, this is such a sad story and sad memory from the past. You can turn this sad memory into a learning experience and make it disappear. I think that you have learned a good lesson from this terrible action, and it seems if you keep this lesson in your heart forever, that sad memory will cease to haunt you.

On a happier note, I have a collection that has no value at all, except for the words and dates that I write on each one. – Becky)

CHAPTER 28

A Collection Popping with Joy

Becky

*"Give every day the chance to become
the most beautiful day of your life."*

*– Mark Twain
(Author, "Huckleberry Finn")*

Corks and memories.

I have been enthusiastically collecting corks for many years. Each one memorializes a happy event. On each cork – in thick, black ballpoint pen – I write the dates, places and names of friends who shared a bottle of wine or prosecco with us. Then, my favorite thing to do is place them randomly around the house to create a totally unexpected surprise when I come across them. Usually, they prompt me to send a quick email to a friend from long ago, asking them for updates. My emails appear out of the blue and usually inspire hilarious replies!

I often warn old friends that they will never get rid of the Civjans. "We are like gum on the bottom of your shoe," I tell them. The truth is that without my corks I probably would never think to write a note when there is no holiday card waiting to be sent.

My very first corks were tossed into a glass vase and placed on a shelf in the cupboard. I never thought to look at them. It struck me one day that my cork collection was "silly stuff sitting on a shelf" and I came very close to tossing them out. That is when I decided to tuck them into places around the house, like a desk drawer, my nightstand, or a cabinet in the laundry room. The problem with this expanding collection is that we seem to be having way too many Happy Times, Happy Hours. It seemed corks were popping up all over the place all the time.

Then, one day I came across a cork from a little winery that was close to our house when we were living in Italy. We liked their wine, and went there often, and as soon as I picked up the cork I remembered the first day we visited. We were buying some wine and stood talking to the owner who showed us his impressive wine cellar. We ended up standing in his office which was beautifully decorated. Old wood from wine barrels that had been polished to a beautiful sheen had been used throughout the room on the flooring and cabinets. One wall was artistically embellished with Corks!

A great idea popped into my head! I could build a wall of corks in some out-of-the-way place, like along the garage wall. Or maybe I could string them and hang them like beaded curtains! If I kept thinking, I would surely come up with an idea to display them in an eye-catching fashion. It was beginning to look like I could have my wine and keep my corks too. All I needed was a little creative thinking to turn them into art!

* * *

(Becky. That's similar to my shadow box collection, although I wish I had met you earlier so that I could have learned to label each item, as you did with your corks. A pretty sharp observation, wouldn't you say? Speaking of sharp, did your mother ever tell you, "Don't run with scissors!" The thing is, when you're little, that advice doesn't make sense, because kids' scissors are always those dull, blunt-tipped student kind. All of them ... All 50 of them! Read on and wonder. – Tony)

CHAPTER 29

A Night of 'Shear' Anger

Tony

*"Red tape will often get in your way.
It's one of the reasons I often carry scissors!"*

Richard Branson
(Business magnate and astronaut)

A pair of folding scissors.

*I*t was just a tiny pair of scissors that hung on my key chain, always there in case I needed to cut out a coupon, remove a string from my shirt, or impale a rabid squirrel. Once I even lent it to my daughter so she could cut out a dress pattern for a Barbie doll she was dressing. The point is, those scissors were not only useful, but also versatile. It folded in such a way that the two cutting edges slid into each other so that I wouldn't injure myself while fumbling for my house keys in the dark. It was a handy tool, and it was always at the ready, to serve my every cutting need.

Unfortunately, it fell victim to fear.

My wife Mary and I had tickets to attend a rock concert in Allentown, Pennsylvania. It was held at the PPL Center, home of the Lehigh Valley Panthers professional hockey team. We made our way through the streets around the arena crowded with concert-goers on their way to the show. We parked in the multi-level garage nearby and walked to the front gate – excited with the anticipation of a night's pleasure, listening to the music of one of our favorite bands.

When we got to the entrance, we were faced with an annoyance that had grown throughout the country at similar music venues – the interrogation, and the search.

"Do you have any weapons on you?" asked a man with a metal-detecting wand in his hand.

"No," I said.

He ran the wand over my body, and I half expected him to utter the incantations of a faith healer from some sort of cult. The wand beeped when he drew it over the front pocket of my jeans.

"What's that?" he asked.

"My car keys," I said.

"Let me see them."

Exasperated, I drew them out of my pocket and handed them to him.

"What's this?" he asked.

"It's a pair of fold-up scissors," I said, and I showed him how they worked.

"That's pretty neat," he said, "but you can't take that in with you."

"Why not?"

"It's a weapon."

"Whaaaat? You're kidding! They're just a miniature pair of scissors."

"But you could stab someone with them," he said, looking at me as if that was my intention all along.

"Well, what do I do with them then?"

"I have to confiscate them," and he indicated a barrel next to the table filled with knives, all kinds of metal things, even nun-chucks, and a string of firecrackers, although I didn't see any guns, which made me worry.

"Okay," I grumbled, and I started to wiggle the scissors off my key chain loop. "I'll pick them up on the way out then."

"No, they're being confiscated. You won't get them back."

I glared at him, and in that moment I considered actually using my tiny tool of destruction on him! Was it my imagination, or did he suddenly change into a rabid squirrel? More reasonably, I thought about leaving – not even bothering with the concert. But I had paid good hard-to-come-by money for the tickets, and Mary really did want to see the show. Then I thought I could leave, hide the scissors under a bush or even dig a little hole in the flower bed near the door, and retrieve them later. But that seemed like too much bother. Besides, the concert was about to begin. Although I didn't pay a lot for those scissors, I did like the way they were designed. Maybe I could find another pair just like it somewhere.

"Okay," I said, "but this is ridiculous."

"It's the rules," he said, but I wondered if they did this at Carnegie Hall in New York City.

I handed them over – gone for good.

We went into the arena, found our seats, and stayed for the entire concert. I did not enjoy it. I don't even remember who was playing.

Over the next few days, I looked for another pair of scissors to replace those "stolen" from me, but I couldn't find any. I did purchase a similar pair, but they weren't the same. Even though they could fold into a nice tight package, they weren't quite right and became more of an irritating reminder of that disappointing night than a useful tool.

Thinking of tiny scissors, however, does hearken me back to when my son Ian was in second grade while I was stationed with the Army in Nuremberg, Germany. One day, Mary and I were cleaning out his closet and we found an old cigar box that we had never seen before. Inside were more than 50 pairs of children's snub-nosed safety scissors, designed for tiny hands – school scissors!

"Where did you get all these?" Mary asked Ian.

He sheepishly admitted that often, after art class, he would walk around the room collecting scissors.

"Did you steal these?" Mary asked.

"No, Mom, they were just laying there. I thought we could take them home with us."

"Why so many?" an astounded Mary asked, more intrigued than angry.

"I don't know, Mom. They were just there, so I picked them up."

There it was, Ian's Achilles heel. He was a closet kleptomaniac!

"Well, tomorrow you're going to take them back and apologize to your teacher."

"Ah Mom, do I have to?"

He did, but I can't help wondering about his poor teacher exasperated with the loss of all those scissors, thinking perhaps they were going to the same place where that single sock goes after all the laundry has been folded (By the way, it's in the lint filter, where the cremated remains of all lost socks go). It also makes me wonder about where my confiscated scissors ended up. Perhaps the guy who took mine has a collection of them in an old cigar box in his closet? Although that image is a bit quirky, it brings on a sadness in me, the result of my frustration and anger at all those who in the past did bring real weapons to concerts, thus creating the need for security guards to protect crowds from terrorists bearing tiny scissors.

Still, whenever I think of both experiences – the ruined concert and Ian's inexplicable scissor collection – I smile, because those scissors aren't just stuff that disappeared, they return to cut well-fitting stories from the whole cloth of memory.

*   *   *

(That is sad, Tony. You mentioned that they were 'just' a little pair of scissors, and that is exactly what they were to everyone except you. They were no longer just a pair of scissors since they had become part of you over the years. They were a practical, indestructible tiny source of reliability, and I would not have handed them over so quickly. I think I would have buried them under a rock in the parking lot, stuck them in a shrub, or put them under a trash bin, and dashed out at the end of the concert to retrieve them. – Becky)

CHAPTER 30

Self-writing Memoir

Becky

"When you put down the good things you ought to have done, and leave out the bad ones you did do well, that's Memoirs."

– *Will Rogers*
(Beloved American humorist)

Collection of calendars.

I joined a memoir writing group because I like to write and I like to join groups. Our leader and author of "The Memoir Revolution," Jerry Waxler, inspired us to put pen to paper and document the stories that make up our lives. Whether it was to share with family today, or for great-grandchildren to discover in the future, we were all ready and eager to begin.

Everyone seemed to be very good at coming up with topics to read in class every week. I could not. Nothing about my life was particularly interesting to me. My family was fine, but I thought there was nothing unusual or interesting to write about. I liked growing up in Washington, D.C. with so many places to go and things to do, but that read more like a travelogue than a memoir.

One day I decided to open the long blanket chest that I have used to store all my calendars dating back to the 1970s. Every year I bought the largest wall calendar I could find, with big blank squares for every day of the year. Then, every night I would quickly jot down something interesting, or worth remembering, that happened that day. If stories required more space, and I thought they were worthy of more detail or commentary, I would continue onto the back side of the page. At times I was forced to staple additional sheets of paper onto the calendar for those events that were clearly above and beyond a normal everyday day. Some writings are scribbles that require a magnifying glass and patience to read. The days displaying good penmanship are usually the more boring, uneventful entries. "I really should have typed a log instead of ending up with all these calendars and a big blanket chest in which to store them," I thought one day. But I didn't think I would have the discipline to sit down and write a synopsis of each day in a journal. My wall calendars were hanging in clear view so we could check what activities were planned for the entire month. At the end of the day, to scribble something noteworthy in that blank space was fast and easy. It was a habit. I did it all my life without even thinking about it.

One day, not very long ago, I was thumbing through these oversized calendars looking for a topic to write about for Jerry's class. It hit me like a bolt of lightning; This WAS my memoir! It had written itself while I was busy living my life! I began thumbing through the pages faster, and it began to remind me of those little cartoons (flipbooks or kineographs) where the animation is drawn on individual cards that you flip very fast to make the characters run down the road! My calendars were exactly like that. Flipping through them showed me running right through all my many years.

I wrote about seeing my own newborn child and mentioned that everyone's little unique personality, the one that carries them through life, is visible in that newborn nursery. I wrote about taking our babies out in strollers and then graduation day for each of those babies. I wrote about meeting each grandchild for the first time; pets and their stories, including a ferocious parrot we owned in Panama; many happy celebrations, and teardrop-stained notes describing overwhelming sadness.

"Well," I thought, "I can put down my pencil right now. If anyone is interested in my life, they can just flip through my calendars."

While thinking of documenting my life in this "kineograph" fashion, I wondered if it would be possible to watch a baby transform from a newborn to a child celebrating a first birthday using this same technique. I picked up a photo album and began to marvel at how remarkably different a child looks from the time they are born until their first birthday. The change is so dramatic that first year. How could we not see those changes as they are happening? It seems incredible that we look at that baby every day all day long, never seeing any change at all. I stared at the photo taken in the newborn nursery and then at the first birthday photo and tried to imagine how this complete transformation could take place and go unnoticed!

What I should have done when each child was born, was to take a quick photo, then take the same photo of that child in the same pose every single day for the entire year. Imagine during that first birthday celebration, flipping through all the photos very fast and watching the dramatic change take place before our eyes! This method is often used to show flower buds gradually opening, and then in full bloom.

"Why not do it with people?" I thought.

I missed my chance with all my babies, so I asked my husband if I could take a picture of him every day so we could watch him get old. He declined. I needed an enthusiastic participant. It would have been much easier with a newborn.

Tucking away my photo albums and kinescope daydreams, I stood staring at my treasured calendar-stuffed blanket chest. It was 2019 and I was forced to decide what items we would transport to our tiny motel-size house in Florida. Our Florida decor is very modern. An antique blanket chest is not. I began to hyperventilate. Is it possible that my blanket chest gets left behind? Where would I store my calendars to keep them safe? I have a whole lifetime invested in those pages and my whole life story told.

It took me only minutes to reach the decision that I could not make that decision yet. I will see if I can photograph them and have them filed digitally on the computer. That will be on my list of things to do when I have nothing to do. Somehow, I knew that day would never come. Meanwhile, I am stuck with a big monster pile of stuff that takes an entire piece of furniture to store. The only way to eliminate it would be to write the entire collection of days into one "simple" memoir. So here I am sharpening my pencil and getting ready to write "A Simple Story of My Life."

*   *   *

(Becky, I can't believe it! You also have a pile of calendars. How remarkable. Mine are the pocket kind, and they're stored in a Tupperware box ready for me to mine for story ideas to write. The only problem is that the tiny, day-by-day squares can hold only two or three words. I guess that's why I started keeping a journal, also from the 1970s. One of these days I'll get around to sifting through those pocket calendars for tales of my life that might have otherwise been lost. Some day. In the meantime, it seems as if life runs away with my time. Sigh. Oh well. Speaking of running away. Follow me on this next true tale. It's a doozy. – Tony)

CHAPTER 31

Runaway Stuff

Tony

*"You can only run away from a house.
Home is something you run toward."*

*– Michele Jaffe
(American author, "Bad Kitty"*

A pack of candy cigarettes.

*W*e were living in West Pittston, Pennsylvania, just a few blocks from a corner grocery store, back when there were corner groceries. We called it "The Candy Store," because the counter top held a line of heavy glass jars filled with penny candy. Each time I went there, I used a bit of the change my mother gave me to buy hard candy cinnamon suckers, Sugar Babies, chocolate mints, or – my favorite – caramels.

One Saturday in 1958, my mother sent me to fetch a loaf of bread. I was about 8 years old. I counted the change into Mr. Ambelton's hand, then noticed a new kind of candy in one of his jars — small boxes of candy cigarettes with red tips, as if they were already lit and ready for smoking. I fished two packs out, slipped another dime into Mr. Ambelton's hand, and walked out with my prizes. As I reached the door, he called out, "Don't forget your bread, Tony!" I sheepishly went back to pick up the loaf I had left on the counter. To an 8-year-old, candy is more important than bread.

It was mid-afternoon when I got home, I handed my mother the bread.

"Did you get anything for yourself, Sweetie?" she asked, knowing I had.

"Yes! Look what I found," and I showed her my cigarettes.

A longtime smoker of Pall-Mall cigarettes (four packs a day!), my mother frowned, but only said, "That's nice."

Nearby, my younger brother David perked up and came running across the kitchen.

"Can I have some, Tony?"

"No, they're mine. I went to the store, so I get to keep them all. Besides, you're too young to smoke." I was reaching for some excuse to keep every last one of them for myself.

Mommy intervened, saying, "Now, Tony, you can share with David, can't you?"

"No!"

She frowned again. "Then maybe you shouldn't have any of them." She put out her hand and said, "Give them to me."

Hesitating, but realizing I had no choice, I turned them over. Then she put one small box of four into her left hand, and one in her right, and handed one to David and one to me. I was outraged, and the blood boiled to my face as I ran up to my room, clutching only half of what was rightfully mine.

About an hour later, my hurt feelings had simmered into a cold rage. I grabbed a jacket, and my single pack of candy cigarettes, and left the house, intent on running away from home.

"I'll show her," I muttered, and for an instant a quick slap of regret hit me, then it was gone. I started walking.

I had no destination in mind, but the nearby Susquehanna River always was one of my favorite places to go when I wanted to be alone. I headed down to the river, turned left at the narrow park that hugged its banks, then right, across the bridge with its low concrete walls, and into the sister city of Pittston.

I had never been this far on foot before. I just kept walking, aimlessly, not worried about a destination, angry at my mother, angry at my brother, angry at my home. I turned left and followed a road north of the city, which began to peter out: from shops and tall buildings, to mom-and-pop storefronts, to row houses, to cottages and open spaces, to woods and farmland. I kept walking, following my anger, with the dark creeping up behind me.

Late afternoon marched into short shadows and black spaces between the cones of light that splashed on the road surface from occasional streetlights above. I kept walking, but my pace was slower. Every once in a while, I would stop and take in my surroundings, and wonder if there were beasts in the bushes, waiting to pounce on me.

"Maybe I should go home," I said, giving up my courage. But as I trudged along, no end in sight, tired and too alone, I finally surrendered up my anger and screamed "Mommy!" But there was no answer; no one to hear my fear.

I turned around and retraced my steps, but somewhere along the way, I missed my turn, getting even more lost. I turned again, retracing the steps I had just retraced and turned around again. Which way was home? I had no clue. I decided that if I ran, I might catch up to a landmark more quickly. I ran. Where's Pittston? Where's the bridge? Where's home? I ran faster, now sobbing and calling out my mother's name more urgently. Then I stopped.

I went to clear the tears from my eyes, trying to calm myself, and my hand brushed the pocket of my shirt where I had stashed my share of the cigarettes. It was just like the pocket on Daddy's shirt where he kept his L&M cigarettes, not candy ones – 20 in a pack (He smoked two packs a day!). My pack held just four. All of Daddy's shirts had square cornered shapes stretched into their pockets from years of carrying those hard packs of his brand. I wanted to be like Daddy – strong.

I reached into my pocket for my candy cigarettes. With two fingers, I drew out a single stick, chalky white with its red tip, gripped it between my index and middle fingers, and raised it to my lips. I sucked on the chalky candy. It tasted sweet and good, but it made me cough a little due to its dryness. Still, it seemed to calm me down well enough for me to admit to myself, "I need help."

Turning around one more time, I went back to a farmhouse I had just run past. I went up to the door and knocked, but I wanted to run again. I turned to go — too late. A woman with a kind face, and wearing a daisy-decorated house dress, opened the door, looked down at me, and said, "Hi there, little one. You look lost." I reached out, grabbed her behind her thighs, pulled myself close, and bawled, "Mommy!"

When she extricated herself from my grasp, she held me at arm's length, looked into my tear-stained face, and exclaimed, "You ARE lost, aren't you! Come in. Let's warm you up. Are you hungry?"

I nodded and followed her into the kitchen where the rest of her family had been sitting down to eat. She explained that I was lost and hungry, and the man of the house placed another chair between their two children.

"What's your name, honey?" the woman asked. "Do you know where you live?"

"Tony. Tony Nauroth. I live in West Pittston."

"You're a long way from home," she observed. Later I was to learn that I had walked 15 miles, not counting all the steps I retraced.

My mother had taught me how to remember our address. A long time ago she had said, "Just think of the city of Philadelphia and three ones in a row." I looked into my new guardian angel's face and said, "One Eleven Philadelphia Avenue," adding, "I'm lost."

"Yes, I know, Sweetie."

I felt better, perhaps because she used the same word – "Sweetie" – as my mother did earlier in the day when she asked me if I bought candy for myself.

The woman heaped some mashed potatoes and a hot dog on the plate the man had put in front of me. She handed me a napkin and a fork. I smiled and looked at her dress. I decided that daisies were going to be my favorite flower.

"Now you eat up. We'll get you home. Okay?"

"Okay."

The couple went into the next room, and I could hear low murmurs of serious talk. As I ate, I grew more comfortable with the girl and the boy beside me. We talked some. They asked what school I went to (Linden Street Elementary in West Pittston) and wanted to know how many were in my family (Ten, counting me, my four brothers, my sister, my mother, my dad, and two grandmothers). They brought out some toys, and we played a little. I had almost forgotten about the candy in my pocket. Suddenly, the package fell onto the floor.

"Ooh, can I have one of those?" the boy asked.

I hesitated, then pulled the three remaining sticks out and gave one each to my new friends, and the last one to me. As we "smoked" I wondered why this felt different from when I refused to share with David. I tossed the empty pack into a nearby waste basket.

Hours went by. Then the father came into the living room where toys were scattered all about and said, "It's time to get you home, young man."

I don't know how they found my family, and I don't know what happened behind the scenes, but we all piled into their station wagon and drove away. When we passed a fork in the road, we turned right.

I recognized it as the place where my sense of direction first failed me. Soon we passed more houses, shops, and tall buildings, all lit up to fight against the dark. I could see the bridge lights up ahead, and, as we crossed into West Pittston, I peered down to where the city lights danced on the ripples of the river. I worried about coming home so late.

Within minutes, we pulled up in front of my house at 111 Philadelphia Avenue. The car came to an easy stop, and I opened the door to hop out.

"Thank you, ma'am, and you too, sir. I'm home now. Thank you."

"We'll walk you to the door," said the man.

"You don't have to do that. I'm home now." I didn't want my parents to know I had been so lost I had to ask for help. I didn't want trouble. And I knew they would be angry, and I didn't want these new friends to see them get angry at me.

"I know," the man said, "but we need to talk to your parents."

I had lost this battle; it seemed like it was a whole day of lost battles. We crossed the lawn, went up the sidewalk steps, and then the wooden porch steps to the front door. The man rang the doorbell. The door opened immediately and my mother went down on one knee, gathered me in, and pulled me close to her breast. We both broke out into a dissonance of sobs, happy sobs this time. I noticed she wasn't wearing daisies. My father stood behind her, shook the man's hand, and they started to talk about my ordeal. We all moved into the recreation room, and the grownups continued their discussion.

My siblings clustered around me, wanting to hear every detail about my adventure, and offering opinions on what the extent of my punishment would be. I'm sure they were disappointed when none came.

When David heard that I no longer had any cigarettes, he left the room and returned with the pack Mommy had given to him. Holding them out, he said, "Here Tony, you can have these back."

"No thanks," I said. "I don't need them."

* * *

(Tony, you describe so perfectly being lost and then being even more lost. I was reading and reliving a similar experience I had when I set out to return a puppy my friend had given to me after school in third grade, but my parents said I could not keep it. Crying, I headed out around dinner time having only a vague idea of where my friend lived. Darkness will never be as dark as it was that night. And that feeling of fright and impending doom is traveling down my spine even as I type this note. It may be a good thing to experience being lost and then more lost in the dark as a child. After that, very few things ever frightened me. Oh ... and Tony, I'm glad you gave up the cigarettes too!

Now, I am walking over to my bookshelves to see what I can find to read. – Becky)

CHAPTER 32

Cleaning Bookshelves and Discovering Me

Becky

"Books can change your life. Some of the most influential people in our lives are characters we meet in books."

– David McCullough
(American historian)

Cleaning bookshelves.

*I*f ever you want to see how much you have changed over the years, go to your bookcase and look through your collection. I decided recently to clean out some of the books that have been sitting untouched for many years. This is not a task one decides to do while writing out a "to do" list for the day. My secret nudge to get me started is to log on for a pick-up date for donations to several favorite charities.

For this morning's pick-up I cleared out closets, knick-knacks, shoes, clothing, and books. The closets told me how trendy my clothes can be; the knick-knacks reminded me of the many places we have lived and traveled. The books told me exactly who I am and how much I have changed!

"Who IS this person?" I wondered as I flipped through endless pages of Bob Dylan song books, volumes of philosophical ideas from Aristotle to Sigmund Freud, and everything anyone would ever want to know about the inside workings of corruption in government. It seems I spent years obsessed with the search for spiritual enlightenment, healthy diet tips, exercise routines, cleaning advice, and how to raise perfect kids in an imperfect world. Some advice was worth its weight in gold. Some advice was rejected within minutes after reading. Some books held secrets to living my life that have made me … me!

As a student and as a young adult I developed a keen interest in how government works and how a society can grow if a perfect balance exists. Maybe listening to relatives talk about growing up under communist or Nazi regimes made me value my great fortune of being born into this land of opportunity and freedom. Maybe growing up in Washington, D.C. fed this interest in government. I remember our yearly school trips to the Archives Building to read the words written in those great documents and composed by brilliant statesmen who were carrying out the ultimate experiment; to create a government "OF, BY and FOR the People with Liberty and Justice for All."

The world I grew up in was so very different than that of my grandchildren. In grade school we said the Pledge of Allegiance and the Lord's Prayer every day, and I heard each word inside my heart. I may have changed in many ways, but my allegiance to the ideals that were written in our Constitution and the Bill of Rights never wavered.

Over the years I lost interest in books about health and diet. The information keeps changing, and for me, to stay healthy means to simply keep moving! And when it comes to eating, everything is good in moderation ... even potato chips!

I have been dusting my collection of books for such a long time and it is easy to see how much I have outgrown some of them. Much like articles of clothing that no longer fit or are quite dated, many beloved authors grow stale over the years. And then there are authors whose books I read when I was nineteen and today I still find myself thinking about what they taught me. I laugh as I write this because Kurt Vonnegut was my guru for many years. I loved his books when I was nineteen, and I still think about them sometimes. Of course, I am not the same person I was at nineteen and do not so readily agree with him now, but I do like to quote him from time to time. I especially like his quote from "Mother Night" – "We are what we pretend to be, so be careful about what we pretend to be."

I don't toss books because they are old, I toss them because I have *grown away* from them. They have lost their value to me personally. I never regret having read the ones I toss. It is a sign that my mind is growing, busily creating a philosophy of my own.

The best lesson I have learned is that we should not rely on one person's words or one ideology to carry us through life. Every day we should be gathering information to form our very own, unique Self to guide us along.

"So," I say, "today this is who I am... But don't BLINK!" – because I believe the quest for information continues, and that every day of life gives us a new opportunity to learn new things and re-establish ourselves as vibrant individuals. These are my thoughts in a nutshell.

And one more thing – I refuse to get old! Old to me is much like the books I am tossing off my shelves. They stop growing after they are published. The world changes but these books never change their words or ideas.

This is my philosophy of life. And it wasn't until today while cleaning the bookshelves that I put these deep feelings about who I am into words. This has been a very good day.

*   *   *

(Becky, I have a journal that I've been keeping since 1976. It has grown up to 38 volumes. At the end of each one, I keep lists of books I have read, books I intend to read, and books I'd like to read, but which I know I never will. I am a lover of books, and now I know that you are, too. Thank you for this insight. But I have a question. Why is it that so many books fill table after table of library sales, flea markets, and garage sales? Do those stories and all that information just keep on going? And if it does, where does it go? Or is it simply a never-ending story? – Tony)

AFTERWORD

Tony writes ...

"All the snow has turned to water,
Christmas days have come and gone.
Broken toys and faded colors,
Are all that's left to linger on."

– From John Prine's "Souvenirs"
(American folk singer and songwriter)

When we took on this project of writing about "Stuff," I thought I was tackling an inanimate object, like a football dummy used to train gridiron athletes. I thought I would wax eloquent on how stupid it is to collect things. I thought stuff was an anchor, not a sail, and therefore worthless in getting me across the seas of life. Stuff, I thought, was just so much ballast, and I was prepared to make fun of it. To fling it over the side of my ship of life. Boy, was I wrong!

What I didn't realize was that even the words I use to pen a letter, fashion a family Christmas email, or construct my memoir are just so much stuff. Yet, they are the DNA of stories, and stories are what we all pass on to the future. They are the embodiment of history and culture, and they abound with humor and sadness, winning and losing, the good and the bad.

I now know that words, and the stories they build, have a value that we often access through our senses. I touch a toy, a souvenir, a tool, a gadget, and even just a rock, and I recall a cherished moment. This isn't stuff; these are touchstones to memory. I shouldn't be surprised, then, that the term we use to describe these things – "keepsakes" – has the word "keep" in it.

So what if someday my stuff goes into the trash, off to a second-hand shop, donated, or simply lost. While it's here, and regardless of how much or how little I have, it's all mine.

When I pick up the chunk of the Berlin Wall that I plucked from that barrier with my own hands, I remember being in Germany at that time. I recall the emotional bubble that burst in my chest when that wall came tumbling down; I felt the HALLELUJAH! of joy. When I look at the miniature wooden chipmunk displayed in its shadow box on my living room wall, I remember swimming at Promised Land State Park so many summers ago, where chipmunks abound; building sand castles on the beach and longing for girls in bikinis. When I touch the dried petals of a rose pressed between the pages of my journal, my heart leaps because that was the rose I pinned to my wife's dress when I took her to her high school prom (before we were married). And when I read that journal today, the stories rush out, calling to me "Hey, do you remember when …?"

And I remember.

What I've learned, then, in working with Becky on this project, is that stuff can be good, but it's got to be the right stuff. More to the point, I now know that it's not the stuff that is eternal, it is the story behind each piece of stuff that goes on forever, and therein lies hope for the future.

AFTERWORD

Becky writes ...

Our stuff can be found all around us. It is in closets, on shelves, in our homes, cars, and in our pockets. "I've got to get rid of this stuff!" echoes in our minds, and then minutes later we are distracted from our declared mission. So, in the end we are stuck with lots of it, and that, I think, is what gives *Stuff* a bad name!

There is a big difference between all that clutters our space and the meaningful items we collect. *Good Stuff* mysteriously pulls us into a fleeting 'flashback to the past' that brings meaning to our lives, a smile to our lips, and warmth to our hearts. And how strange it is that over time this "matter" that we collect can transform from mere objects to overwhelmingly marvelous feelings that appear not only in our heart, but in our soul as well.

When Tony and I began this project on Stuff, I didn't think there was much I could learn about the topic we chose. I felt like an expert in this field, having collected and discarded tons of it continuously through the years. I did want to know what makes some stuff meaningful and if there is one basic ingredient that is found in the stuff we cherish. It may vary from one person to the next, but for me it was obvious – people. There is something very special that we find in those we love, and they bring that special quality to every moment we share together with them. We spend our time making memories and these are the ones we hold onto forever.

Writing this book has been a remarkably fun and exciting experience. Tony and I began with friendship and an idea. We mixed it with enthusiasm and commitment; and soon thereafter, we joyously set off on a writing spree that brought lighthearted laughter and deep introspection into every waking hour.

Writing gives us a chance to abstractly think our words and then see them appear before us. It is, to me, the most introspective and rewarding activity, and I would encourage everyone to pick up a pencil and write. We have gyms in every community to keep us in good shape. Thank heavens there are writing groups that do the same for that often-neglected muscle – the one we have sitting on our shoulders.

ABOUT THE AUTHOR

Becky Civjan, always writing.

Becky Civjan was born in Washington, D.C. in 1948. She lived just a short bus ride from the Smithsonian, the White House, U.S. Capitol Building, Art Museums, the Library of Congress, and so many other national landmarks. It was a "Thinker's Disneyland" with so many exciting things to inspire her youthful exuberance.

One of her teachers in elementary school taught the class to keep a daily journal and told them to note something new they had learned every day. It was so much fun she decided to continue this routine forever, writing daily blurbs on wall calendars which will eventually find their way into digital form, or perhaps a children's book memoir about "One Lucky Lady."

She moved to Silver Spring, Maryland, and met a very cool guy named Ralph, whose father was an Army dentist and the Chief of Dental Research at Walter Reed Army Medical Center. They both headed off to the University of Maryland. Ralph wanted to be a Forest Ranger, but, at Becky's urging, he headed to dental school instead.

Upon graduation, Ralph enlisted in the Army Dental Corps to serve his country, save some money, practice dentistry, and later settle down and open a dental practice. At least that was the plan. But sometimes life doesn't always follow "The Plan." Instead, they spent more than 29 years as a military family living in interesting places, finding great friends, and making memories.

Ralph retired from the military in December 2002. They then lived in Vicenza, Italy for six wonderful years where Ralph worked as a contract dentist for the Army and NATO Forces. They enjoyed traveling all over Europe, and Becky kept her quest of learning something new and exciting every day. She earned a Certificate of Italian Studies from the University of Maryland overseas.

The Civjans have three children: Their older son is a structural engineer and professor of Environmental Engineering at the University of Massachusetts, Amherst, and lives with his wife in Florence, Massachusetts. They have a son and a daughter.

The younger son lives in Seattle, Washington with his wife and son and works at the University of Washington.

Their daughter and her husband both work at the lab in Los Alamos, New Mexico. They have a daughter and a son.

"Just when we thought life could not get any better, we became grandparents," Becky says. "I am astounded by the richness of life, and I consider myself to be a fortunate 'victim' of good luck! How else could I possibly end up with such amazingly smart and talented children and grandchildren?"

Embracing life-long learning and a love of writing is something both Becky Civjan and her co-author Tony Nauroth have in common.

ABOUT THE AUTHOR

Tony Nauroth, on the trail of a story at Lake Titicaca, Bolivia.

Tony Nauroth is a retired U.S. Army Master Sergeant who had served with the "Stars and Stripes" newspaper in Europe, as a photojournalist with "Soldiers" magazine out of Washington, D.C., and as the loftily-titled "Chief of Army Newspapers" out of the Pentagon. He also served in Panama and throughout South America, as well as North Carolina, Massachusetts, and New York City.

Tony is married to the former Mary Ellen Opdyke, who understands the absence of stuff more completely than he does. They have two children. Bethany, now 50, lives outside a small town north of Reading, Pennsylvania. She and her husband Joel have lots of stuff (including their daughters, Greta and Renate). Their home is pretty much disorganized (including Greta and Renate!)

Son Ian, 46, lives with his wife Laura Herschel in Philadelphia. They have a house that's neat as a pin, so there's no telling how much stuff is there. They have no children, but they do have two cats – Carly and Lucy – who seem to get into all kinds of stuff.

Tony holds a Bachelor of Science Degree in Liberal Arts from the State University of New York's External Degree Program. He still doesn't know what "Bachelor of Science in Liberal Arts" means, other than it seems to be an oxymoron.

When he retired from the Army, Tony joined the staff of "The Express-Times" out of Easton, Pennsylvania and later wrote for "The Morning Call" out of Allentown, followed by the very local "Valley Voice" based in his home borough of Hellertown. Those newspapers have either disappeared, or shriveled into ghosts of themselves on the Internet.

Tony is working on his memoir, "An Accidental Soldier," focusing on his 20 years in the service. He is also working on several other writing projects, including "Love Letters from Leo" – based on 17 letters his father wrote to his fiancee (Tony's mother) from 1946 through 1949 – and this book.

Tony spends his free time playing guitar in the band "The DeadLiners" and feeding his backyard squirrels, who constantly "stuff" themselves with peanuts. His life is simple; his thoughts are wild.

ACKNOWLEDGMENTS BY BECKY

This journey through *"The Eternal Life of Stuff"* would never have taken place without the encouragement and support of so many. The Waxler writing group created an atmosphere that made writing a passion. Sharing ideas with this great group of friends has made me aware of how very much I love to put thoughts to paper. Words – it is all about words.

Conversation is the way we share ourselves with others in a very personal way. A book of "conversations," then, seemed appropriate. Our favorite mementos are so very often filled with thoughts of people and the rich conversations we have had with them.

A big thank you to those in my family who never roll their eyes and have always been kind when I bounce random ideas in their direction. To my dear husband, who doesn't mind a new adventure every day or eating dinner at midnight, and to friends who have miraculously appeared, bringing such joy and creating wonderful memories; I am indeed a lucky lady.

And to Tony, who I sincerely admire because of his honesty, his witty humor, and his ability to lasso my flightiness and unleashed energy, and calmly steer them into this book. Our book that has taken the form of a "written conversation" is the product of sharing ideas and working together. This teamwork exploring "The Eternal Life of Stuff" feels like the beginning of yet another conversation waiting to happen. (Are you ready, my friend?)

Tony and I are total opposites, so I learn something new every day by watching him. I found out what a very organized, methodical person does with his day. He types up lists and check sheets and sends them in emails, with expectations that a person living in my world would know what to do with them!

ACKNOWLEDGMENTS BY TONY

I would be remiss not to also thank Jerry Waxler for his invaluable guidance. He has been a large-hearted mentor and friend.

To my wife, Mary. I could not have come this far without her love, or her lessons. And to my children and grandchildren, and those yet to come. You are the future and my inspiration for co-creating *"The Eternal Life of Stuff."*

There is a myriad of those who contributed to this project, often without even knowing about it. This is especially true of all the women I have worked with in my writing career. Each has a small but important part in this book because what I found to be true is that women are wonderful teachers and more adept at language than men.

I'd like to thank my granddaughters – Greta Geisinger, 16, for being such an avid reader; and Renate Geisinger, 14, for her robust embrace of everything life puts before her. They are who I thought of with every chapter I wrote. After all, this will become part of their inheritance.

To Wilma Koss, Becky's dear friend, an educator and writer, who brushed through our book, lending her time and talents to put the finishing editorial touches on our manuscript, like a house painter putting the final coat on the trim. I've never met you, Wilma, but I admire your skills and am in awe of your contributions. Thank you.

There's also a background voice from a woman who I didn't know very well when we both attended Tunkhannock Area High School in 1968. Alice Hadsall-Smith has been something of an earworm, always whispering "Write it right!" to my brain. A published author herself, Alice is helping me with my major memoir, "An Accidental Soldier." Although she had no part in the actual production of "The Eternal Life of Stuff," she always remains my inspiration.

And then, of course, there's Becky. Becky Civjan, a fellow traveler through life in the U.S. Army, and yet I didn't meet her until later in life when she came upon me unexpectedly. But that's the way she is ... unexpected. Her energy – pure energy – always seems to fire like lightning off clouds of ideas to strike the ground in unexpected places and often in confusing ways. She is inspiration incarnate. Remember the children's classic tale, "The Little Engine That Could?" Becky is the little engine that could ... not ... be ... stopped!

This then is really Becky's book. All I did was turn energy into matter.

THE LAST WORD

Becky and Tony never stop talking, or writing. If you enjoyed "The Eternal Life of Stuff"... Stay tuned. There are two more books on the way!

# # #

Printed in the United States
by Baker & Taylor Publisher Services